*150 Encouraging
Devotions for Women*

Journey
into
Grace

Darlene Sala
Bonnie Sala, Luisa Reyes-Ampil

BARBOUR BOOKS
An Imprint of Barbour Publishing, Inc.

Print ISBN 978-1-68322-285-9

eBook Editions:
Adobe Digital Edition (.epub) 978-1-68322-511-9
Kindle and MobiPocket Edition (.prc) 978-1-68322-512-6

Published by Barbour Books, an imprint of Barbour Publishing, Inc., P.O. Box 719, Uhrichsville, Ohio 44683, www.barbourbooks.com

Our mission is to publish and distribute inspirational products offering exceptional value and biblical encouragement to the masses.

 Member of the
Evangelical Christian
Publishers Association

Printed in the United States of America.

Praise for Journey into Grace

"Food for the journey: we all need to pack a little something for the trip, and these daily selections will provide perspective, comfort, and inspiration for every turn on your path. Darlene always packs a lot of wisdom into every writing and conversation. This latest offering, joined by Bonnie and Luisa, is food for the soul."

—Lisa Ryan, Christian TV Host / author, speaker, and ministry ambassador—InTouch Ministries

"This is not your typical book of devotionals. This is for real. Darlene, Bonnie, and Luisa are powerful women of prayer and faith in Jesus Christ. The power of the One in whom they trust radiates from the pages of challenging, thrilling, and encouraging personal examples. I loved reading it! Dive in; 'stretch your tent curtains wide, do not hold back; lengthen your cords, strengthen your stakes, for you will spread out to the right and to the left' (Isaiah 54:2 NIV)."

—Janet Broling, author of *What Can One Woman Do?* and *How to Reach Your City*

"What I like about this devotional is that the authors didn't paint themselves as Christian Superwomen, the perfect Proverbs 31 women who never struggle in any area of their lives. This devotional can speak to every woman—from the baby Christian who is about to buy her first Bible to the president of the Women's Fellowship."

—Beng Alba-Jones, freelance writer and editor

"*Journey into Grace* is filled with honest and thought-provoking devotionals that are easy to read, full of truth, and are easy to apply to our lives. They don't sugarcoat the challenging situations that so many of us face, but they don't lead us to despair either. The authors always guide us to our true source of hope, Jesus Christ, our Lord and Savior. In their words, He provides 'handfuls of grace in pain-filled valleys.' This book will help you to find and hold onto that grace."

—Cathy Burns, cofounder of HomeWord ministry

"Darlene, Bonnie, and Luisa make an inspirational, inter-generational team. Their insights are precious. Mother, daughter, and friend, they shine together. Though separate in their life journeys, country of origin, pain, and spiritual backgrounds, they bond with sisterhood wisdom for us all."

—Miriam Neff, author and founder and international president of Widow Connection

"The passion for Jesus and knowledge of the Word of God, along with a practical and purposeful way of life, make *Journey into Grace* an inspiring, challenging, Biblically sound and relevant devotional work. *Journey into Grace* is filled with rich nuggets on each page that draw the reader into a deeper knowledge and understanding of His grace for all circumstances."

—Dr. Peggy Banks, Global Ministry Director for TransWorld Radio Women of Hope

Introduction

The day each of us came into this world we began a journey. Now, the journey is always a mixture of good and bad, *sometimes very good and sometimes very bad*. The twists and turns along the way often threaten to undo us. Sometimes they actually do.

But we have a resource in the sustaining riches of God's grace that can help us not only survive these hard times but eventually thrive—because He will bring us into a more intimate relationship with Himself than we would ever have had if everything in our lives had gone smoothly.

Walking with you on the journey is the purpose of this book. I've invited two special women to walk with us. My daughter Bonnie Sala and my colleague and friend Luisa Reyes-Ampil have come to know the strength and the sweetness of God's grace along their journeys. Bonnie never dreamed that her path would include betrayal, pain, and despair. Luisa made her way as a single mom starting over in a new culture, raising twin daughters to young adulthood. Together, as we have shared our THRIVE: Journey into Grace seminar around the world, we have seen women respond in relief to the realization that we all share the same struggles.

Our prayer is that these readings, these snippets of truth we've stumbled onto in quiet moments with Him, will encourage you to press into Him daily as you travel your own journey into grace.

Darlene

Acknowledgments

Whenever several authors join together to write a book, you have a unique opportunity. Three authors. Three life messages. Three perspectives. Thank you, Bonnie and Luisa, for contributing with me openly from your unique journeys into God's grace to make this book "real." Every time I read what you write, I feel that I know you better. Big hugs to you both.

Another big thank-you goes to Annie Tipton, senior acquisitions editor at Barbour Publishing; Jessie Fioritto, copyeditor, for helping us say what we really intended to say; Courtney Coffman, for taking the manuscript through the editorial process so expertly; Krista Maxwell and Emily Morelli, for your design touches to the inside and outside of this book; and to Yolanda Chumney, for typesetting the book and making the words just right on the page.

And thank you, dear reader. If it weren't for you, we wouldn't be writing books! All three of us pray that God will use these selections to make your path smoother as you travel on your journey into grace.

Darlene

On Our Way. . .

"My grace is all you need.
My power works best in weakness."

2 CORINTHIANS 12:9 NLT

Contents

God's Will or Mine?

*A decision we have to
make daily (maybe hourly)*

Choosing Wisely!
By Bonnie Sala

*So be careful how you live. Don't live like fools,
but like those who are wise. Make the most of every
opportunity in these evil days. Don't act thoughtlessly,
but understand what the Lord wants you to do.*
EPHESIANS 5:15–17 NLT

Distraction: Something that takes your attention away from what you're supposed to be doing. It used to be that we said we were "driven to distraction," but in this twenty-four-hour-a-day connected world, distraction is our constant companion. And a constant temptation. Of course there's nothing wrong with media, social and other types. In many ways they've made our lives richer and more fun. But there is so much information, so many images and so much stimulation, that before you know it, important time is gone, wasted. We've focused on *perfect*-looking people, homes, families, and lives. We've been tempted to covet and become dissatisfied. Or worse.

When it comes to making good choices about the activities and influences I let into my life, I love the advice written long ago by the mother of nineteen children, who was known to flip her apron over her head in the midst of chaos to be alone and pray. Susanna Wesley (1669–1742) is said to have shared these guidelines in a letter to her son John. When "you judge the lawfulness of a pleasure take this rule: Whatever weakens your reason, impairs the tenderness of your conscience, obscures your sense of God, or takes away the relish of spiritual things; whatever increases the authority of your body over your mind, that thing is sin."

I can tell you my reason is definitely weakened, my thinking affected, when I am spending too much time online. Confession: I admit to following fashion blogs. But after my eyes have taken in touched-up image after image after image of beautiful (and young) women who have pretty much starved themselves and had teams—*yes, teams*—of people working on their hair and makeup, the woman who looks back at me in my mirror makes me cringe! I don't remember that my Father is a king, that I was handcrafted to bring Him glory, to love Him and others, or that " 'people judge by outward appearance, but the LORD looks at the heart' " (1 Samuel 16:7 NLT). I long to be and have things that God has not ordained for me.

Reflection

Do you find yourself constantly checking your phone or media device? What drains away your time?

Conversation with God

Lord, help me to be careful how I live, making choices and using my time for activities that strengthen me and make me more aware of You! Speak to me through Your Spirit when I become distracted and stumble into sin.

A Battle for the Throne

By Luisa Reyes-Ampil

I saw the Lord sitting upon a throne, high and lifted up;
and the train of his robe filled the temple.

ISAIAH 6:1

If there ever was a well-known historical battle over a throne, it was between Mary, Queen of Scots, and her cousin Queen Elizabeth I of England, two women who never actually met but just exchanged letters through their envoys. Nevertheless, the alleged discovery of a plot to kill Elizabeth for the throne of England eventually led to Mary's trial, imprisonment, and execution.

However, the truth is that we ourselves often fight a "battle for the throne" in our households each day. I know my ex-husband and I did. He gave me carte blanche in handling our children. Whenever they disobeyed rules and I deferred to him, he usually said, "Listen to your mom and do what she says!" So whenever he did exert authority, they didn't listen. I was already reigning on the throne! Sometimes I still don't feel like giving up my authority and end up in arguments with my now-adult children.

Satan also bids for a throne, creating betrayals and conflicts between families and between nations. And of course, Satan's saga is thousands of years old, and he has his own cavalry to help him fight his dirty battles. He fights to gain the seat of authority and power in our lives as well. But we don't have to give in. Even if we don't feel spiritually mature and powerful, God's Word says, "Little children, you are from God and have overcome them, for he who is in you is greater than he who is in the world" (1 John 4:4).

In the final chapter of history, though, this is what will be:

> *Behold, a throne stood in heaven, with one seated on the throne.... From the throne came flashes of lightning, and rumblings and peals of thunder, and before the throne were burning seven torches of fire. . .and before the throne there was as it were a sea of glass, like crystal. And around the throne, on each side of the throne, are four living creatures. . . . , And day and night they never cease to say, "Holy, holy, holy, is the Lord God Almighty, who was and is and is to come!" (Revelation 4:2, 5-6, 8)*

In the end there will be no battle for the throne, for there is only one throne—God's! To be coheirs, however, we need to make sure that we are indeed true loyal members of His royal household.

Reflection

Who is sitting on the throne of your heart right now?

Conversation with God

I praise You, O Lord, for making me a rightful coheir with other believers. Help me to see You always as my true King!

God's Plan and My Hair

By Bonnie Sala

For the creation was subjected to frustration,
not by its own choice, but by the will of the one who
subjected it, in hope that the creation itself will be
liberated from its bondage to decay and brought into
the freedom and glory of the children of God.
ROMANS 8:20–21 NIV

Different. That's how I felt from the time I was old enough to look in a mirror and compare myself to everyone else around me. It was. . .the *hair*! Clearly, hair was supposed to grace the head like smooth silk, flowing down onto the shoulders in perfect order. But what was the stuff sprouting from my head, rebelliously twisting and turning in no order at all, fuzzy and frizzy?

My three-year-old mind thought, *It's my brain waves! Hair is obviously brain waves that grow out of your head and MINE are different from everyone else's!!* Every Saturday night, my poor mother tried rollers, pinning it down, and even taping it to my cheeks, but to no avail. The next morning it would be coiling this way and that, doing its own thing again.

Sure, God knit me together in my mother's womb, but for fifty years I was convinced He had dropped a few stitches while knitting! My hair did what it wanted, and for the most part, I think I really did, too. Although careful to "do the right thing" and live the "Christian life" on the outside, I was fairly sure that God's will for my life and my will were going to line up pretty well. And then. . .they didn't.

No, the circumstances of my life and my frustration weren't what I would have chosen, but in the midst of struggling with great pain, in surrendering my will I did experience liberation! I found that the One who allowed the pain could be trusted. I came to actually know Him—which enabled me to trust Him and experience living in glorious freedom.

Yes, my hair is frustrating. Yes, God's will for me may include agonizing frustration. But I found freedom when I accepted that God's plan for my life was going to be far richer and more meaningful and that it was going to work itself out very differently than I had envisioned. And with a different hairstyle. And. . .it was good!

Reflection

What have you been struggling with God over?

Conversation with God

Lord, help me to submit all my frustrations, pain, upset plans, my will, to You today and let me experience the glorious freedom that only You can give!

When You're in Transition
By Darlene Sala

*Trust in the LORD with all your heart, and do not
lean on your own understanding. In all your ways
acknowledge him, and he will make straight your paths.*
PROVERBS 3:5-6

After working as a newscaster in Asia for four years, Ali Smith Kennedy made plans to return to the US. Because she had no idea where she would live or what she would be doing in this next phase of her life, she felt some unease about the change. Her friend counseled her that she was like a trapeze artist who had let go of one bar and was soaring through the air reaching for the next bar. She advised Ali to study what a trapeze artist needs during the transition when she is suspended in the air between the two bars.

Ali says she learned three things were needed:

* Trust—she needed to believe that God was guiding her even in this period when she felt she was all on her own, with no security to hold on to.

* Timing—any trapeze artist knows the ultimate importance of timing. If you don't let go at the right time, you won't be in position to catch the next bar when it comes within reach. Either holding on too long or letting go too soon will cause you to miss the next bar. Ali realized only as

she let go of her present position could she be in the place God wanted her for her next place of responsibility.

* Holding position—fear can cause a trapeze artist to panic, flailing her body so that she cannot soar out to where the next bar is waiting for her. She must keep her body aligned and ready to catch the bar at the moment it comes within reach. When we're in an insecure place in our lives, we need to hold steady, not panicking because we have nothing to hold on to. After all, our circumstances may have changed, but God hasn't changed.

Are you in a period of change in your life right now? Don't panic. Instead, trust, watch for God's timing, and hold your position. He will help you catch the next bar.

Reflection

What do you need to do right now while you wait for God's timing in your life?

Conversation with God

Lord, I can't see where I'm going. Please help me trust in You until You show me what's next.

Out of Control!

By Bonnie Sala

But I trust in you, O LORD; I say,
"You are my God." My times are in your hand.
PSALM 31:14–15

As a young adult, I was one determined woman. If I wanted something, I worked harder than anyone else to get it. I used to carry around a little clipping of this quote by Mark Twain in my wallet: "The miracle, or the power, that elevates the few is to be found in their industry, application, and perseverance under the prompting of a brave, determined spirit."[1]

I had plans for my life (and a boatload of pride). I pretty much knew how life would go because I would *make* it go that way. Of course I prayed about my plans, but if I was truthful, I would have had to say I was praying that I'd get my own way.

Then came the black cloud of infertility. *I'd make a plan! I'd see the best doctors, scrupulously follow protocol. Shots, pills, procedures!* But there we were: me, my husband, and the doctor, floundering beneath that big, black cloud. Yes, this was out of my control.

"It's easy to start believing that we are in control, especially when things are going our way. We see ourselves," observed

---

1 Mark Twain, quoted in "Pass It On: Inspiring Quotations," Values.com, accessed December 3, 2016, http://www.values.com/inspirational-quotes/4167-the-miracle-or-the-power-that-elevates-the.

Deborah Howard, "as masters of our own fate. We can carelessly glide through life that way until when? Until we are brought face to face with a situation *definitely, obviously* and *completely* out of our control. Our tendency to self-sufficiency can only be overcome when our situation is beyond our sufficiency."[2]

Definitely, obviously, completely out of control. *I* was out of control. Today I can look back with gratitude for having been brought to my knees, asking for forgiveness for my arrogance. "Ironically," says Howard, it is when we are on our knees, "that we are our strongest because we acknowledge God as our only true source of strength. And there is no strength mightier than God's."[3]

My two sons came in God's perfect timing. I am overwhelmed by these gifts of God, the work of His hands. They represent His immense and illogical love for me. They will always be reminders of who He is and who I am not.

Reflection _____

Have you struggled to control your own life?

Conversation with God _____

God, bring me to the end of myself that I might find the beginning of You and Your perfect strength.

2 Deborah Howard, *Sunsets: Reflections for Life's Final Journey* (Carol Stream: Crossway Books, 2005), 140.

3 Ibid.

A Legacy of Love and Grace
By Luisa Reyes-Ampil

> " 'Well done, good and faithful servant. . . .
> Enter into the joy of your master.' "
> MATTHEW 25:23

Nicole Nordeman's song "Legacy" spoke volumes to my heart when I first heard it. The big question it asks? *How do you want people to remember you when you are no longer around?*

I ponder that question often in my family life. I ask myself the same thing in my public life—as I write books, as I speak at various engagements, as I meet old and new friends.

I was labeled a rebel growing up. It was hard for me to obey my parents if I wasn't given an explanation as to why I had to do something. It was the same thing for me at school. What a surprise I must be today to everyone as I write and speak of God's authority in my life!

I developed a strong work ethic and easy camaraderie with colleagues at all levels when I started my career. That was the first time I thought of a legacy—how did I want people in the workplace to see and remember me when I have moved on? Was I going to be easily forgotten or remembered as someone who helped others accomplish their goals? I smile when I see some of my ex-colleagues' messages like "My experience was made better having you as my boss" and "I will never forget you, Luisa."

As a single mom, my own family thought I was too strict and demanding. Even my kids groaned under our home rules. My daughter Christelle, who is now a teacher, said one day, "I can't understand why students are having a hard time completing homework! My sister and I didn't have that problem and did well in school." Godly discipline and responsibility taught and instilled early in life was the answer.

As God allows me today to minister to people in many ways—through books, speaking, counseling—I have become more intentional about my life. I always examine my motives. Is this about being in the limelight? Or, is this about sharing God's Word and how it has impacted and transformed my life? If the answer is the latter, then I know it's about God's legacy of love and grace!

Reflection

How do you want to be remembered when you are no longer on this earth?

Conversation with God

I pray that one day I will hear "Well done, good and faithful servant" from You, Lord!

A New Heart

By Bonnie Sala

*"And I will give you a new heart, and I will put a new
spirit in you. I will take out your stony, stubborn
heart and give you a tender, responsive heart."*

EZEKIEL 36:26 NLT

One of the things I love about God's Word is that, besides being
a light to our feet and a lamp for our paths (Psalm 119:105), it
presents to us real people with real flaws and shows us how God
deals with us.

Take Saul, for example. The tallest and most handsome
man in Israel, he had come across the prophet Samuel while out
searching for lost donkeys. "Don't worry about those donkeys
. . .for they have been found," Samuel told him. "I am here to tell
you that you and your family are the focus of all Israel's hopes"
(1 Samuel 9:20 NLT).

Saul was more than a little shocked: "I'm only from. . .the
smallest tribe in Israel, and my family is the least important of
all the families of that tribe! Why are you talking like this to
me?" (v. 21 NLT). But the next thing you know Samuel gave Saul
a kiss and anointed him with oil. And as Saul turned to leave,
"God gave him a new heart" (1 Samuel 10:9 NLT). But Saul went
home and kept the whole thing a secret.

So, the big coronation day arrived. Samuel called all Israel to meet before the Lord and receive the king they had asked for. And when the actual moment arrived. . .Saul was nowhere to be found! So they asked the Lord, "Where is he?" And the Lord ratted Saul out: "He is hiding among the baggage." There, probably crouching on the ground behind bags and bundles, was the man who stood head and shoulders above anyone else: God's choice to be king over all His chosen people. "This is the man," said Samuel, "the LORD has chosen as your king. No one in all Israel is like him" (1 Samuel 10:24 NLT). Hiding among the baggage.

Are you hiding from the purpose God has for you among the baggage of your life? Even after God has called us into relationship with Him, we may still experience fear and doubt, but yes, even if we stumble (keep reading Saul's story in 1 Samuel), God can still use us!

Reflection _____

Have you asked God to give you a new heart? Have you said yes to letting Him put His perfect plan into action in your life?

Conversation with God _____

God, I thank You that You have the power to use me for the purposes You have planned for my life. I offer myself to You today.

A Cleansed Conscience

By Luisa Reyes-Ampil

*"I myself always strive to have a conscience
without offense toward God and men."*
ACTS 24:16 NKJV

In the Disney children's film *Pinocchio,* the little wooden puppet's friend, Jiminy Cricket, taught Pinocchio to "always let your conscience be your guide." Choosing right seemed black-and-white then, but since childhood, we've all put some mileage on our consciences! I read an essay that presented and contrasted four different states of man's conscience—our consciences may be weak, defiled, seared, or cleansed.

A *weak* conscience is apparent when we're easily persuaded in decision making. We sometimes make wrong choices based on other people's advice or by copying their behavior, also known as peer pressure. Many adults give in to a weak conscience, too, when they entertain the lusts of the flesh. If we realize that we need to have a strong spiritual foundation, that each decision we make requires godly choices, we won't suffer from a weak conscience.

A *defiled* conscience is one that's morally blemished, impure, having its purity corrupted—nothing positive at all! Evil is prevalent today, and it's not uncommon for people to say, "It's all relative!" If our minds are not clearly influenced by and set on godly standards, our consciences may be so defiled that even wrong choices seem right. Our consciences become defiled when we know right but do not acknowledge it.

Then there's the *seared* conscience. Seared items are popular on fine restaurant menus today, like my favorite, seared ahi tuna. Searing is done by putting meat or fish on a really hot pan or flaming grill for a short time. If left too long on the heat, though, the meat turns into a dry, hard, black blob, making it unfit to eat. A seared conscience happens when one continues to do evil in God's eyes. You turn the MUTE button on—or maybe switch off the POWER button—to silence the Holy Spirit, resulting in a hardened heart.

But we do have a gracious and merciful God, who can turn any kind of conscience into a *cleansed* one if we humbly ask for His forgiveness. As the hymn goes, "What can wash away my sin? Nothing but the blood of Jesus!" And if we have been washed by Christ's blood, we must remember to please God with our thoughts, words, and deeds—burying our weak, defiled, or seared consciences in the past.

Reflection _____

What is the state of your conscience?

Conversation with God _____

Help me to realize the sin in my life so I can be cleansed from unrighteousness and please You. Thank You for a fresh start every morning!

The Power of a Choice

By Luisa Reyes-Ampil

Approve the things that are excellent,
that you may be sincere and without offense.
PHILIPPIANS 1:10 NKJV

"Your life today is the sum total of all the choices you've made up to this point," wrote Joe Stowell. "In any given situation, we have a whole continuum of choices—ranging from really rotten choices, to the mediocrity of average choices, to choices that are good, and then to those that are excellent. God wants to move us across the continuum, past our natural impulses, all the way to excellent choices."[4]

I know I have made some rotten choices in my life that taught me hard lessons. As for the mediocrity of average choices— definitely, yes! When I am too lazy to even pause to pray for God's will even though I know His way is best, there I go. Perhaps I get by with no one hurt and...problem solved. Thank You, Lord, for sparing me!

When it comes to the choices that are good and those that are excellent, it's these choices that I sometimes grapple with. Often they have been hard decisions, causing me to ask the Lord why I had to make them. I see the benefits of some of my good and excellent decisions but sometimes can't see what I

---

4   Joe Stowell, "Dreams or Choices?" *Our Daily Bread*, February 18, 2011, accessed March 14, 2017, https://odb.org/2011/02/18/dreams-or-choices/.

have gained from others. For instance, after my husband left me, I chose to remain single for almost two decades while I was raising my daughters to focus solely on raising them. That was an excellent, if hard, choice.

In the Old Testament book of Daniel, chapter 3, you can read about the excellent choice Shadrach, Meshach, and Abednego made to stick to the one true God. They were thrown into a fiery furnace because of their decision, but God protected them in a miraculous way, turning King Nebuchadnezzar's heart to worship God.

Excellent choices are sometimes hard to make, but not impossible. Some results we may see only when we get to heaven. But making them now definitely allows us to be a true witness for the Lord Jesus Christ!

Reflection

Make a list of all the choices you need to make right now and evaluate which ones you can turn into excellent choices for the Lord's glory.

Conversation with God

Help me, Lord, to be a true witness for You by standing up for what is right. In moments when I doubt and feel helpless to choose the right way, give me courage and strength.

An Unexpected Freedom

By Bonnie Sala

"If you try to hang on to your life, you will lose it.
But if you give up your life for my sake, you will save it."
MATTHEW 16:25 NLT

If I were honest, I would have to say that my prayer for much of my life was this: I wanted to get my own way. My way would be an easy one, devoid of challenges, one that my flesh could handle just fine with a few encouraging Bible verses thrown in. Of course, God loved me too much to allow me to go on pretending that He was my Lord while tightly clenching the steering wheel of my life.

"When we choose to stay in control, we are, in effect, choosing to be controlled by someone or something other than God . . .although it seems safe and logical to be in charge of your life, being in charge becomes a heavy, lonely responsibility,"[5] explained Cynthia Heald in her book *Journey to the Heart of God.* It was indeed a heavy responsibility. But, my flesh undaunted, I tried to "save" my life and help those close to me save their lives as well. Instead, my life was lost to trying and then trying harder. It was hard to breathe.

"Your Father graciously offers to take your life, protect you, strengthen you, and comfort you on your journey," Heald writes,

---

5   Cynthia Heald, *A Woman's Journey to the Heart of God* (Nashville, TN: Thomas Nelson, 1997), 27.

and He did circle tighter and tighter, waiting and wooing. I had a death grip on my life and the lives of those I loved. The giving up, the dying, didn't happen in a day, but when I asked, He slowly helped me loosen my grip until my hands were raised to Him. It was necessary for me to learn, as author Corrie ten Boom did, to "Hold everything in your hands lightly, otherwise it hurts when God pries your fingers open."[6]

On this side of surrender there is a lightness and a quietness to the work of God in my life that is so unlike my frantic ways. What a relief it is to leave the responsibility of control for both my life and the lives of those I love to Him!

Reflection

Have you relinquished full control of your life to God? What are you holding on to?

Conversation with God

How I do want to give up my life for Your use, Father. If I'm not there yet, please draw me to the point of complete surrender.

---

6   Debbie McDaniel, "40 Powerful Quotes from Corrie Ten Boom," Crosswalk.com, May 21, 2015, accessed November 30, 2016, http://www.crosswalk.com/faith/spiritual-life/inspiring-quotes/40-powerful-quotes-from-corrie-ten-boom.html.

Blowing It

By Luisa Reyes-Ampil

The way of a fool is right in his own eyes.
PROVERBS 12:15

Alicia Silverstone cannot outlive her memorable statement made after her hit movie *Clueless*: "I think that the film *Clueless* was very deep. I think it was deep in the way that it was very light. I think lightness has to come from a very deep place if it's true lightness."[7]

But what if your misstep is more serious? How about Steve Harvey's flubbed announcement of the winning contestant during the Miss Universe 2015 pageant? Many people, especially the Colombians, still dislike him after their beauty queen was awkwardly de-crowned for the rightful Miss Philippines to uncomfortably wear and parade it before the clapping audience.

And after the world applauded Caitlyn "Bruce" Jenner, who publicly transitioned from a man to a woman at the age of sixty-five, the news of panic attacks and regrets over the sex-change decision followed.

The Body Joy Project is "a feminist art collective challenging the notion of beauty standards and promoting self-acceptance."[8] They attempt to somehow help women recover from the shame of rape, violation, or anorexia by painting and exhibiting their nude bodies.

7 "Top 30 Most Stupid Quotes by Celebrities," Daily News Dig, accessed September 17, 2016, http://dailynewsdig.com/30-stupid-quotes-by-celebrities/.

8 "To Be Brave," *Coast Magazine* (May 2016): 32.

I watch and listen with my mouth and eyes wide open in shock. I shake my head and wonder why most people are applauding and cheering this kind of "world-breaking" news. "Who cares?" I hear from the younger generation. "Times have changed and you are living in the past!" some claim. Even worse, some people think they have a license to sin because the Bible says, "Where sin increased, grace abounded all the more" (Romans 5:20).

"Has not God made foolish the wisdom of the world?" (1 Corinthians 1:20). The time will come when each of us will have to account for our deeds. Let's align our actions now with God's Word so our accomplishments won't be counted as foolishness in God's eyes.

Reflection

What worldly beliefs are you holding on to that run counter to God's Word?

Conversation with God

Dear God, save us from ourselves and the foolishness of this world, and help us to make the right choices each day.

The Challenge
By Luisa Reyes-Ampil

The heart of man plans his way,
but the LORD establishes his steps.
PROVERBS 16:9

"Live by Your Own Plan," was Blue Shield of California's challenge in their newsletter. One of the leading health-care insurance companies, Blue Shield called for their current and prospective subscribers to take charge of their own medical coverage. If you want a lower deductible and copayment, you could pick a plan with a higher premium. A lower premium plan resulted in a higher deductible and out-of-pocket expense.

All of us want to live by our own plan. That's why the insurance company picked that advertising catchphrase. Toddlers don't want to hear the word *no* from anyone, so they bite and scream at playmates and throw temper tantrums in front of adults. Teenagers hate being told what to do in their homes and in schools, so they cuss at their parents and teachers and slam the doors to block out the voices. Employees are unhappy when supervisors don't let them do their jobs the way they want to, so they grumble and complain to their coworkers. Married couples continue to live as individuals because they are used to their old ways and "there is no way someone can change me." Consequently divorce and annulment cases are increasing in number.

But living by our own plan does not work because there is always fine print that we either overlook or forget—the consequence of our actions. We find enjoyment in the present moment until our plans go awry—actually, against God's will—and then we suffer pain, disappointment, and every negative emotion you can think of. The good news is that God's grace and mercy definitely can intervene because of His great love and forgiveness. God can help you get back on His plan. Simply admit your failure, ask Him to forgive you, and follow His Word.

You may call it old-fashioned or passé, but living by God's plan is still the best. " 'For I know the plans I have for you, declares the LORD, plans for welfare and not for evil, to give you a future and a hope' " (Jeremiah 29:11). How can you ever go wrong when you surrender and allow God's plans to supersede yours?

Reflection

Billy Graham once said, "Do you want to know what God's will is for you? It is for you to become more and more like Christ. This is spiritual maturity, and if you make this your goal, it will change your life."[9]

Conversation with God

Heavenly Father, I praise and thank You that if I seek You with all of my heart, You will be there to direct and to guide me. I surrender my plans to You!

---

9 Billy Graham, quoted on "Quotes about God's Will," Goodreads, accessed November 13, 2016, http://www.goodreads.com/quotes/tag/god-s-will?page=3.

Thy Will Be Done

By Bonnie Sala

*He went on a little farther and bowed with his face to
the ground, praying, "My Father! If it is possible,
let this cup of suffering be taken away from me.
Yet I want your will to be done, not mine."*
MATTHEW 26:39 NLT

Hers is a story so many of us can relate to. The loss came only a
few short months after becoming aware of the new life that grew
within her. She learned that a little one that had been asked for,
had been prayed for, would not be born.

Hillary Scott, of the hit trio Lady Antebellum, worked with
two fellow song writers to put her grief into words and song,
bringing her raw, honest pain and questions to God. When
she grappled with her loss, bad feelings and her conflicting
confidence that God is good, she could only come up with the
words from Jesus' own prayer right before He went to the cross:
"Thy will be done."

Scott explained, "Having things that go on in your life you
think are going to be really awesome and then all of a sudden, it
feels like the carpet is ripped out from under you. . . I've prayed
about something in my life and felt like God had answered that
prayer and then the way in which it was answered looked a lot
differently than I thought it would. . . I was questioning and

confused, and all the while knowing though that ultimately. . . His will is what's best."[10]

I love Scott's poignant song because it reminds me that I can take pain that makes no sense, a broken heart and even questions about God Himself and His Word...straight to the lap of my Heavenly Father. We see Jesus' own example of pleading with His Father to remove the pain of the Cross. Our Father has given us invitations in the Psalms to express sorrow (Psalm 137), disappointment and rejection (Psalm 74), anger (Psalm 140) despair (Psalm 22) and depression (Psalm 88). He is big enough for it all and He welcomes us.

Reflection ————————————————————

Have you been able to take your painful questions to God and yet say, "Thy will be done"?

Conversation with God ————————————

God, thank You that You are God and I am not. Thank You that You welcome my sorrow, disappointment and rejection, anger, despair, and depression. Gently bring me to my own point of welcoming Your will for my life.

10 Staff. "Hillary Scott's Beautiful Music Video to 'Thy Will' is Full of Truth." Wayfm.com. Accessed April 30, 2017. http://www.wayfm.com/content/music/hillary-scotts-beautiful-music-video-to-thy-will-is-full-of-truth/.

Your Spoonful of Diamonds

By Darlene Sala

"Come to me."
MATTHEW 11:28

Ann Voskamp tells of losing the diamond from her wedding ring somewhere coming in from the barn and evening chores. A 2 mm, .05 carat diamond—the only precious stone she'd ever owned.

Then Voskamp points out that "if you multiply the volume of a .05 carat diamond by the number of weeks in a full lifetime of 90 years (4,680), it adds up to just under one tablespoon."[11] That means if you live to be ninety years old, all the weeks of your life add up to a spoonful of diamonds. Just one spoonful of diamonds.

While losing the diamond from your wedding ring is very sad, it doesn't compare with losing a portion of your life. Diamonds can be replaced. But your life cannot.

Dear sister, do you understand that God has put you on this earth for a reason—primarily because He wants to have fellowship with you every single day? You bring glory to Him by your relationship with Him—not just by what you do. The older I get, the more clearly I see this. Accomplishment is not God's primary goal for you. What He wants for you is intimacy with Himself.

---

11 Ann Voskamp, "How to Mine Your 2015 for Unexpected Diamonds" from *A Holy Experience*, January 6, 2015, accessed March 27, 2017, http://annvoskamp .com/2015/01/how-to-mine-your-2015-for-unexpected-diamonds-and-a-giveaway-for-dslr-camera/.

You can have this heart relationship at any point in your day—while working at your job, caring for your child, or deciding what you're going to have for dinner tonight. You can find that intimacy with God when your heart is broken by your husband's infidelity or the funeral of your dearest friend or receiving the doctor's report that your condition is life threatening. God is there, waiting for you. He says, "Come to me" (Matthew 11:28).

You don't have to go through life alone. The One who said, "I will never leave you nor forsake you" (Hebrews 13:5) is waiting for you to turn your life and your situation over to Him totally. Pour out your heart to Him. Lean on Him for all that you need. You don't need to settle for less.

Reflection

If you're going to have an intimate relationship with the Lord, what's the first change you need to make in your life?

Conversation with God

Lord, I want that intimate relationship with You. With all of my heart I come to You right now and turn my life with its problems over to You.

If Only
By Bonnie Sala

The LORD directs our steps, so why try
to understand everything along the way?
PROVERBS 20:24 NLT

If only. If only I had listened. If only I hadn't done that. If only I hadn't said that or *had* said something else. If only I had known that he… If only I could do that over again. Regret, like bitterness, is a prison that we put ourselves in. But the Christian need not live in this prison, for it is a figment of our imaginations, of our flesh. "The LORD directs our steps, so why try to understand everything along the way?" we are asked in Proverbs 20:24 (NLT). But I do try to understand because it gives me a sense of control. Because that's what my flesh is all about. Me. Being in control.

The Christian should list all of her "if onlys" and draw a circle around them, says Pastor Erwin Lutzer. Then, he says we should label the entire circle "The Providence of God, for God is greater than the Christian's 'if onlys.'… His providential hand encompasses the whole of our lives, not just the good days, but the 'bad' days too."[12]

What does God's Word say about my *if onlys*?

* The timing of all events in my life is in God's hand. (Psalm 31:15)

---

12 Erwin Lutzer, *One Minute after You Die* (Chicago: Moody Publishers, 1997), 123–24.

* He has determined where and when I will live. (Acts 17:26)

* God works in "bad" circumstances for my good. (Genesis 50:20)

* I make my plans, but He determines my steps, and His purposes prevail. (Proverbs 16:9; 19:21)

* My future is in His hands. (Psalm 31:15)

* If something is of God, I can't "overthrow" it. (Acts 5:39)

* Any riches or honor in my life comes from God. (1 Chronicles 29:12)

* The timing of my birth and death is set by God. (Deuteronomy 32:39)

When I realize that *I'm not God* and that He is in full control, my *if onlys* seem to lose their power, and thankfully so. Yes, when I've failed, I can come to Him and ask for forgiveness. But I don't need to stay there in regret. The believer lives inside the Circle of the Providence of God. That's a comfort I need to focus on today.

Reflection _____

What *if onlys* have you been imprisoned by?

Conversation with God _____

God, forgive me for forgetting that You are sovereign, for the times I've relied on my "good plans" or been in despair over my failures. Thank You for the comfort of living in the Circle of Your Providence.

The Fight

By Luisa Reyes-Ampil

Return to the LORD your God, for he is gracious and merciful,
slow to anger, and abounding in steadfast love.

JOEL 2:13

"God Fights against Us" was the title of a selection in the devotional booklet *Our Daily Bread*.[13] The thoughts were taken from the book of Joel, and the writer notes that we have seen many heartbreaking and terrifying events worldwide recently. We view beheading videos on YouTube. The death tolls rise in record-breaking earthquakes and typhoons. Russia and other countries wage war against neighboring countries.

How about an acquaintance sending her teenage daughter to rehab? A lot of hurtful, emotional, and disruptive times happened in that girl's life and family before that rehab trip. The daughter's friends all think the mom is wrong for sending her away, even if it was to treat addiction.

Whether the events are personal or worldwide, the question is always in our thoughts: "When is this ever going to stop?" We think that it must be that God is not around to protect us and He is punishing us. Or that He doesn't care and simply forgot about us.

We must remember, though, that even God's chosen people

---

13 Albert Lee, "God Fights against Us," *Our Daily Bread*, August 23, 2006, accessed March 23, 2017, http://odb.org/2006/08/23/god-fights-against-us/.

in the Old Testament times went through so many of these "God is against us" situations. And it always happened when they had forgotten Him after He has blessed them, protected them, and provided for them. Today, many just live the way they want to—without respect for self and others. But we believers know that these things also happen because times are moving closer to the end when Christ will return to earth.

"God against us" often means simply that He is sending us a wake-up call because we have gone astray. In layman's terms, it's called *intervention*. God loves us too much to give us up. If necessary, He will send circumstances where He appears to be against us so we can see that He is stepping in to save us from ourselves and harmful consequences.

Now, I don't want to experience defeat, but I know there is no way I can ever win against the Lord. It would be suicide. Let's not wait for God to fight against us before we stop. Let's bow graciously and return to Him.

Reflection

What hurtful things have recently happened in your life that you need to commit to the Lord and accept as His loving wake-up call?

Conversation with God

As I reflect on my life and the events taking place everywhere, help me to realize that I need to change to make a difference. Renew my heart, dear Lord, so I can be part of the grace and mercy You show to everyone.

Interruptions

By Darlene Sala

Little children, let us not love in word or talk
but in deed and in truth.

1 JOHN 3:18

In her book *God's Front Door*, Jill Briscoe asks, "Do you ever have days where you have all your time wonderfully organized and then you get nothing done as planned because of constant interruptions?"

Briscoe tells about coming to the end of one of those days and waiting impatiently to talk to God that evening so she could start griping about her messy day. She writes, "I had had it all scheduled out and then it began. I no sooner got going when the phone rang, the kids called, the washing machine overflowed, the dog ran away, and a needy person appeared from nowhere and demanded my attention. I hate that!"

She admits that the needy lady didn't fare too well!

I tried to listen to her litany of woes, but I had my eye
on the clock and she caught me glancing at it every two
minutes! She left hurriedly, feeling unwelcome, uncared
for, unloved, and as empty as she came. I felt a twinge of
guilt, but thankfully it soon passed, hurried out the door
of my conscience by all my righteous excuses.

"Well," I assured myself—"it was her fault! She
hadn't made an appointment!"

"I made one for her," a Voice said in my ear! I

jumped. I hadn't seen Him arrive. "You made the appointment?" I asked. . . . And then I blurted out—"But You didn't check with me first!"

"You didn't check with Me either," He pointed out mildly. . . . "She needed you." . . .

"But Lord—You know what my schedule looked like!" I argued.

"You had a choice," He replied. "It's really quite simple. People matter more than schedules, Jill. . . ."

"Oh," I muttered miserably.

He left then. I got to my feet and reached out to Him. . . .

"Please Lord, if it's not too late, send her back to me tomorrow."

"But your schedule's already full of things to do."

"Please Lord—I'll be waiting."

There was a long silence. And He was gone.

She didn't come back—why should she? What did I miss that day? Who else received the blessing of investing in her life? What a loss![14]

Reflection

"Each day is God's gift of a fresh unspoiled opportunity to live according to His priorities."—Elisabeth George[15]

Conversation with God

O Lord, please help me to listen to You and to be sensitive to the needs of the divine appointments You send my way.

14 Jill Briscoe, *God's Front Door* (Mill Hill, London & Grand Rapids, MI: Monarch Books, 2004), 28–31.
15 Elisabeth George, quoted in "Priorities," Daily Christian Quotes, accessed October 27, 2016, http://www.dailychristianquote.com/tag/priorities/.

The Call

By Bonnie Sala

He called you to salvation when we told you the Good News;
now you can share in the glory of our Lord Jesus Christ.
2 THESSALONIANS 2:14 NLT

"He received *the call* to the ministry at age sixteen." "She was *called* to work with disabled children in Africa." For most of my life I've identified the *call of God* with ministers and missionaries. Not the sort of thing that touches the life of the "ordinary" Christian.

Wrong, says Pastor Tim Keller. The call of God on the life of every believer, he explains, is absolutely necessary. And a quick search of scripture backs Keller up. Paul wrote, "He called you to salvation when we told you the Good News; now you can share in the glory of our Lord Jesus Christ" (2 Thessalonians 2:14 NLT). And, "for the gifts and the calling of God are irrevocable" (Romans 11:29). John said: "He calls his own sheep by name and leads them out" (John 10:3 NLT).

"Each person must hear the call of God," Keller explains, and the call comes in power. "God's Call humbles, breaks, disturbs, convicts and shakes us; without it [we] are just nice little idolaters."[16] If God's call has not had this impact on me, I

---

16 Timothy Keller, "Real Security and the Call of God," Gospel in Life (audio blog), April 22, 2001, accessed December 4, 2016, http://www.gospelinlife.com/real-security-and-the-call-of-god-5233.

may be moral and religious, but I am still an idolater, because I will live for my career, my family—something else other than God. I am in a "spiritual death sleep" without the call.

Secondly, God's call is an act of grace. I am not called because I am qualified, but I am *qualified* because the call has come! A human call can't give the requisite qualifications, but God's call does. What He calls me to, I will be equipped to do. God's call is transformational!

God's call is also personally radical and its purpose is to bless others. "At the heart of the Call of God is the surrender of the will,"[17] says Keller. When God called Abraham, He said, "Get out of your country, leave your people and your family and go to the land that I will show you." And Abraham *went out, not knowing where he was going*" (Hebrews 11:8, emphasis added), so that all the peoples of the earth would be blessed (Genesis 12:1–3). Answering requires faith-infused obedience; the impact of my obedience extends beyond myself.

Reflection

I didn't answer the call with "anywhere, anytime, anything" until the idols in my life had been smashed to pieces. Can you honestly say that you have answered the call of God upon your life?

Conversation with God

Father, thank You that Your call on my life comes with power to transform, equip, and radically bless others.

---

17 Ibid.

I've Got Work to Do

By Darlene Sala

So even to old age and gray hairs, O God, do not forsake me,
until I proclaim your might to another generation,
your power to all those to come.

PSALM 71:18

"What age do you have to be before you're 'old'?" my husband likes to ask kids. He gets answers all the way from fifties to "a hundred." I suppose we're really not old until we reach the age when God has no more for us to accomplish on this earth. My mom used to say, "God put me on this earth to accomplish a certain number of things, and right now I'm so far behind, I'm sure I will never die!"

We never want to think of ourselves as being old. Harold and I were shocked to realize a few months ago that on our branch of the family tree, we're now the oldest Sala generation still living! If gray hair means a person is old, however, I suppose I'm old. But with my hairstylist's help you will never see the evidence! In recent days, however, aging has made me realize it's time to give some serious thought to what else I want to accomplish while I'm still on this earth.

The night my dad went to be with the Lord, he asked Harold to read Psalm 71 to him. When Harold read today's featured verse about "proclaim[ing] [God's] might to another generation," my dad asked, "Harold, do you think I've done that?" Frankly, Harold was surprised at the very question. My dad had never been one to ask for affirmation. Harold quickly responded, "If anyone has ever done that, Pop, you have!" for my dad had been in active ministry since he was eighteen—more than seventy years in all. A short while later, he was safe in the arms of Jesus.

On this journey into grace that we're all on, there will come a day when each of us will come to our destination. Before I get there, though, I for one want to have taken every opportunity to proclaim God's might and power to the next generation. That means I've still got work to do. Words to write, people to influence, nudges from God to obey. Do you feel the same way?

Reflection

As songwriter Jon Mohr wrote, "Oh may all who come behind us find us faithful"![18]

Conversation with God

What do You want me to do today, Lord, to share Your greatness with someone who is hurting? I'm listening....

18 John Mohr, "Find Us Faithful," quoted in Reba Rambo Mc-Guire, "Find Us Faithful," *Homecoming Magazine*, June 1, 2013, accessed December 16, 2016, http://www. homecomingmagazine.com/article/find-us-faithful/.

My Will or His?

By Luisa Reyes-Ampil

All things were created by him, and for him.
COLOSSIANS 1:16 KJV

If there was one thing that stood out to me when I read Rick Warren's book *The Purpose Driven Life,* it was this: my only purpose is to fulfill God's purpose for me! And what do I mean by this?

First, I acknowledge the fact that I am God's creation. I didn't just happen to be or evolve from a substance. I am blessed to be the work of His hands and not some scientist's accidental discovery or manipulated laboratory experiment. And like all things created, there are certain attributes that God gave me to make me who I am. And that includes creating me in His own image. "Let us make man in our image, after our likeness," He said (Genesis 1:26).

Second, there is a specific purpose for my being. God did not randomly put me together. He thought of me and knew me before I was formed to fulfill a mission. And that purpose is made and given to me by Him, not dreamed up by me or anyone else. "For those whom he foreknew he also predestined to be conformed to the image of his Son" (Romans 8:29).

Third, my purpose is to worship God as I enjoy fellowship with Him. I was made to give pleasure to the Lord in all that I do—to walk with Him daily and to honor Him through prayers, songs, conversations, decisions, and relationships. That's a 24-7 call! "But you are a chosen race, a royal priesthood, a holy nation, a people for his own possession, that you may proclaim the excellencies of him who called you out of darkness into his marvelous light" (1 Peter 2:9).

I was a bit ashamed of myself when I started thinking of the plans I had made for myself. I know that it isn't wrong to have personal goals and ways of achieving them. But I must first ask if these are in line with *God's* purpose for me. Will they bring Him glory and honor? For it's not my will, but His will that is to be done in my life. Am I willing to give up my plans for His?

Reflection

Do you struggle with giving up your plans for God's plans for your life?

Conversation with God

How wonderful to know that You created me with a purpose! Show me, dear Father, how I can praise You with my life. Thank You that all I need to do is surrender to Your perfect will so You can work out Your purpose for me.

Messages Just for Me

Because His Word is living,
active—and personal

Make a Left

By Luisa Reyes-Ampil

Look to the LORD and his strength; seek his face always.
PSALM 105:4 NIV

My two young daughters and I were visiting a friend from the Philippines at the home of one of her relatives. My daughter wanted to use the restroom, so I asked for directions. The exchange between her brother-in-law and me stuck with me like glue. He said, "Go down the hallway. When you see Jesus, make a left." To which I jokingly, but with intent, responded, "How can you lead people to Jesus and then tell them to avoid Him?"

We are great at avoiding authority figures. Kids shut out their parents by staying in their rooms or tune them out with video games and music. Students dare not look their teachers in the eye for fear of being called to answer a question posed to the class. Employees sit in their comfortable cliques at meetings to surround themselves with friendly coworkers, putting a buffer sometimes between themselves and the boss. We don't even like to greet our pastor after church service because we don't want to be confronted with a personal question, so we opt to be lost in the crowd.

These are exactly some of the things we do with God when we sin against Him. Instead of heeding the Holy Spirit's conviction and leading to stop, we start veering to the right or left because we understand the burden of our shame and guilt. We appear not to hear the inner voice of the Holy Spirit quietly speaking to us about our wrongdoing, reminding us that we have a chance to turn around. We are like little kids pretending to be innocent of our misdeeds until we get so comfortable avoiding God that we are shocked to wake up and see just how far we have moved away from Him.

As Christians, we are to continually walk toward God because we need His direction and guidance. There is no way we can hear and listen to Him if we don't do this. Looking to the left or right will get us off track, which can be detrimental to our spiritual walk. As Hebrews 12:2 (KJV) says, we need to "[look] unto Jesus the author and finisher of our faith."

Reflection

Is your heart sensitive to the leading and correction of the Holy Spirit?

Conversation with God

Heavenly Father, please show me clearly the path to Your Son, Jesus Christ. Put blinders on me to shut out the distractions along the way so I will not go astray and will get to my final destination without unnecessary detours.

Never Lost

By Bonnie Sala

Behold, the eye of the LORD is on those who fear him,
on those who hope in his steadfast love.

PSALM 33:18

The river glistened at the bottom of the valley, its banks framed in dense, leafy bushes that stood much taller than a person. My sister, Nancy, and I were vacationing and fishing with our sons in the mountains; fishing has always been a favorite family pastime. But the fish weren't biting, and Nancy had made her way ahead of me, through the bushes, up the steep trail that eventually led back to our parked car.

Gathering my gear, I headed toward the bushes, not exactly sure where the narrow path was that we had taken through the dense growth. I headed in, thinking I was on the path, but as I floundered this way and that, I couldn't actually see a thing! I had no idea where I was going. Branches scratched at my face; roots threatened to trip me. It was an unnerving, uncomfortable feeling. Somehow, I emerged out onto the other side to see Nancy high above me on the trail. Gulping for air as I climbed, I caught up to her.

"That was funny!" Nancy said. "I could see the bushes shaking as you moved through them. I couldn't see you, but I could see exactly where you were the whole time," she remarked. As we took in the view from high on the hill, I observed what she had seen as my two sons made their way through the bushy little forest below.

I couldn't help but think of God looking down on His creation, on me, as I so often struggle to make my way, totally uncertain of my path and unable to see anything except the crisis before me. From up on the hill, my sister could see exactly where I was. I was never in any sort of danger of getting lost. And I realized, *I am never in any sort of danger of getting lost!* Like Job I can say, "His eye is always on me" (Job 36:7). When I'm unsure, His eye is on me. When I think I'm lost, His eye is on me. When I think I'm all alone, His eye is on me!

Reflection

In what area of your life do you feel unsure, lost, or alone?

Conversation with God

Lord, thank You that You are watching from on high. That You see exactly where I am today, that I am not alone. If I have a relationship with You, I am not lost! Please guide me into all that You have for me. I am Yours.

The Whistle

By Luisa Reyes-Ampil

"And the sheep recognize his voice and come to him."
JOHN 10:3 NLT

The shrill sound had them all scurrying—a woman and the teenage boy and girl—as they were at different sections of the department store. I thought it was a most inappropriate way for my brother-in-law to call his family. I asked my sister Bernadette, "Why do you let Fernando make that sound and call all of you this way?" "It does sound annoying," she admitted, "but it gets the attention of all of us, and we follow the sound and know where to go."

Now, when Jesus was speaking to the Pharisees and raised the issue of the sheep recognizing the shepherd's voice, He was alluding to the fact that these men were leading people astray, for they were not the true Shepherd. He said, "Truly, truly, I say to you. . . . The sheep hear [the Shepherd's] voice, and he calls his own sheep by name and leads them out. When he has brought out all his own, he goes before them, and the sheep follow him, for they know his voice" (John 10:1, 3–4).

It's a fact that a sheep is gentle and timid, needing man's protection. It's prone to wander and get lost, making it easy prey for other animals. Fortunately, the sheep's submissive character makes it highly trainable so that it is possible for the shepherd to give names to the sheep, allowing him to specifically call

58

one from the flock.

The sheep's voice recognition of its master is likened to believers heeding Jesus' voice. He calls each one of us by name to lead us not only out of the pits that we fall into from time to time, but into everlasting life. He goes before us to provide us guidance and light. All we need to do is follow behind Him for protection on the path He has prepared for us.

I get it now how easy it is for Fernando to gather his family wherever they are, no matter how crowded the place is. They don't need to call one another or send a text message so they can instantly gather. They use their own voice-recognition method to come together.

" 'I will whistle for them and gather them in, for I have redeemed them'" (Zechariah 10:8). Jesus is calling us to Himself. Shouldn't we make it easy for Him by responding right now?

Reflection

Are you listening today for the voice of our Shepherd?

Conversation with God

In moments I am not fully focused on You, Lord, thank You that You call me by name.

Introvert or Extrovert?

By Darlene Sala

I cry out to God Most High,
to God who fulfills his purpose for me.
PSALM 57:2

I would have knots in the pit of my stomach when I was headed to an event where I knew I'd be making conversation with people I had never met before. What if I couldn't think of *anything* to talk about?

I had sweaty palms when I was about to address a group of people and saw public-speaking experts sitting in the audience. I had a terrible fear my mind would go blank.

Even as a child, when I had a part to say in the church Christmas program, I'd lose my dinner beforehand or get a raging headache. It didn't take me long to figure out I was an introvert.

As an adult, however, I finally figured out that extroverts don't get a free ride either. Many an extrovert who was the life of the party has crawled into bed after an event only to be haunted with memories of things she said that would have been better left unsaid. "Why can't I just keep my mouth shut?" she asks herself.

One thing is for certain: God did not make us all alike, but He did create you for a purpose—His purpose. He gifted you with exactly the talents and abilities He wants you to have to accomplish His purpose. While each of us can work to improve what we do, it is wrong to try to become someone we are not.

You are a person of value because God created you. He gave you your temperament. He has plans for you. " 'For I know the plans I have for you, declares the LORD, plans for welfare and not for evil, to give you a future and a hope' " (Jeremiah 29:11). Your job is to give yourself to Him, asking Him to work out His purposes in your life. Is that scary for you? It doesn't need to be. Just remember that the One who wants to direct your life gave *His* life for you on an old rugged cross. He loves you more than anyone else could possibly love you. As you pursue His will, He will give you a life that is more fulfilling than you could ever find on your own.

Reflection

"When the Lord makes it clear you're to follow Him in this new direction, focus fully on Him and refuse to be distracted by comparisons with others." —Charles R. Swindoll.[19]

Conversation with God

God, there are many things I don't like about myself. Right now I give them to You. I am going to trust You to guide me and make me a blessing to others.

---

19 Charles R. Swindoll, quoted in "Quotes about God's Love," Goodreads, accessed September 29, 2016, http://www.goodreads.com/quotes/tag/gods-will.

Succulents

By Luisa Reyes-Ampil

*"Whoever drinks of the water that I
will give him will never be thirsty again."*

JOHN 4:14

I got hooked propagating succulents after my late stepdad introduced me to how easy they are to take care of. And because I live in a home that has a paved patio with only a small planter box to use, I started growing succulents and their clippings in pots and all sorts of containers. I also enjoy the varieties I have and watch how they respond to sun and water, moving them around so they can thrive.

Even before California's *Brown Is the New Green* slogan appeared, I was one step ahead in the drought issue with my succulents. Drought-tolerant landscaping is now encouraged in the state, and the city where I live provides free seminars from time to time for its residents to educate them on how to reduce watering of our gardens.

Sometimes we also go through a personal drought. Perhaps we were once excited to read the Word of God and to hear from Him, and now we feel dry because we have neglected to come to Him for "watering." Something has come between us and Him. "The rebellious dwell in a parched land," says Psalm 68:6.

But there is also a large-scale drought. Many public areas once displaying God-related sayings and artwork are now devoid of them. Young people are leaving the church because they are influenced by new worldviews that run counter to the Bible. Even the older and more mature Christians are finding reasons to hop from one church to another, either with complaints about the music, the pastor's age, the message, or other issues. " 'Behold, the days are coming,' declares the Lord GOD, 'when I will send a famine on the land—not a famine of bread, nor a thirst for water, but of hearing the words of the LORD' " (Amos 8:11). *Is this that time, Lord?*

We have a lot to learn from succulents. Succulents have the ability to store water in their leaves and to endure extended periods of drought—and so should we! Storing up God's Word in our hearts and minds will allow us to draw from within when we feel that we are starting to dry up.

Reflection

Are you feeling parched today? It's time to draw from the spring of eternal life.

Conversation with God

Dear Lord, help me to learn how to store Your Word in my heart so I will never run dry.

My Value in God's Sight
By Darlene Sala

*We can understand someone dying for a person worth
dying for, and we can understand how someone good
and noble could inspire us to selfless sacrifice. But
God put his love on the line for us by offering his Son in
sacrificial death while we were of no use whatever to him.*

ROMANS 5:7–8 MSG

Let's say you own a beautiful piece of art—a painting, a gorgeous crystal vase, or perhaps an antique sculpture. How much is it worth? You're probably not sure. There's a way to find out, though. Experts tell us that when it comes to placing value on a beautiful piece of art, that value depends on three things:

1. Who made it
2. How many there are like it
3. How much someone is willing to pay for it

Let me turn that around and ask you, "How much are *you* worth?" The answer can be found by taking a look at the responses to those same three questions:

1. Who made you? The greatest Artist in the universe!
2. How many are there like you? Only one—you are unique.
3. How much was someone willing to pay for you? God was willing to give the very life of His only Son to redeem you from sin and give you a relationship with Himself. That's how valuable you are!!

Don't *feel* it?

In his book *Becoming Who God Intended*, David Eckman pictures God explaining it to us: "My Son is dying for you because you are worth a Son to Me."[20]

Just *think* of it—God says, "*You are worth a Son to Me*"! If you've ever doubted your worth, or you don't know where to go from where you are, or you're losing heart—listen to Father God saying to you, "You are important enough to Me to justify the death of My Son. I want to have a close and intimate relationship with you right where you are."

That's how valuable you are in God's sight. So don't put yourself down. Instead, thank God for His tremendous love for you. Yes, lift your head high and remind yourself that God says you are a piece of art that is amazingly valuable to Him. Really *knowing* that can change your whole day—and your life!

Reflection

Spend a few quiet minutes thinking about that statement: "My Son is dying for you because you are worth a Son to Me."

Conversation with God

You made me, Lord—unique, unduplicated. Thank You for the price You were willing to pay for me.

---

20 David Eckman, *Becoming Who God Intended* (Eugene, OR: Harvest House, 2005), 24.

A Crown of Glory?
By Luisa Reyes-Ampil

But the splendor of old [women] is their gray hair.
PROVERBS 20:29

"Grow Younger" was the title of the cover story of the *Women's Health* magazine. Inside were anti-aging skin and hair secrets that promised to "get you carded in your 30s." Fine if you're only in your thirties, but how much worse if you're long past that. . . and now getting ready to go in the morning takes you twice as long—but you look half as good!

The "transformation" business is booming. Women of all ages and walks of life look to cosmetics and aesthetic surgery to try to stem the tide of time. Wrinkles aside, the most obvious manifestation of old age—and one we hate—is gray hair. The day came when I realized that my own jet-black hair was riddled with random gray hairs, sending me straight to the salon! But I see that the Bible says a lot of good things about gray hair including, "Gray hair is a crown of glory; it is gained in a righteous life" (Proverbs 16:31). So why was I spending money covering up my crown of glory?

Yes, our tendency is to focus on our physical appearance rather than what's more important: our inner beauty. The Bible clearly says that "charm is deceitful, and beauty is vain, but a woman who fears the LORD is to be praised" (Proverbs 31:30). A rich spiritual life is of infinitely more lasting value than beauty!

As I age or mature, I like to keep in mind what my friend Joanie Feuerstein says: "Don't regret growing older—it's a privilege denied to many!" Let's reflect on what Job 12:12 (NIV) says: " 'Is not wisdom found among the aged? Does not long life bring understanding?' " This is what's important: we must learn from the years of experience, both good and bad, and grow in wisdom. We can age gracefully by counting the blessings. . . along with the gray hairs!

Reflection _____

Do you dread growing older? What bothers you the most about physical aging? Can you embrace its blessings instead?

Conversation with God _____

Lord, help me to be excited to "number my days" and to grow in wisdom so I can enjoy my graceful aging. Let me not be ashamed of gray hair in my later years, but to see it as Your crowning glory for me.

Never Mind Me, How Are You?
By Bonnie Sala

Such love has no fear, because perfect love expels all fear.
If we are afraid, it is for fear of punishment, and this shows
that we have not fully experienced his perfect love.

1 JOHN 4:18 NLT

People pleasers. You may know one or you may be one. Nice, helpful people. So thoughtful—they scramble to meet the needs of those they love in every way possible! It's not uncommon for women to be pleasers—the one in the family who makes it all work and holds everything together...for everyone except herself.

"Well, that sounds very godly. After all, 'Count others more significant than yourselves,'" you may say, quoting Philippians 2:3. Or you may criticize the people pleaser, because she "just doesn't have a reverent enough, a high enough, view of God." Or you could accuse that pleasers love the approval of men rather than God (John 12:43).

But there's more here, say Milan and Kay Yerkovich: "In adult relationships, the underlying motivation for being in the helping role and focusing on the needs of others is to reduce one's own anxiety by keeping people close, content, and satisfied. If others are upset, pleasers are distressed as well."[21] The Yerkoviches have found in years of counseling and study that pleasers are likely to have grown up in an atmosphere marked by unhealthy

---

21 Milan and Kay Yerkovich, *How We Love* (Colorado Springs: Waterbrook Press, 2006), 72.

fear and worry, where the world is seen as a dangerous place or where an angry or critical parent dominates the home.

To the pleaser, Jesus says come. " 'Come to me, all you who are weary and burdened, and I will give you rest' " (Matthew 11:28 NIV). Because one day, the pleaser hits the wall. "After pleasers spend a number of years of chronic worry and overgiving, resentment often emerges."[22] And resentment is a heavy burden to carry.

Jesus calls pleasers to begin the process of laying down the burden, the anxiety, a day (or an hour) at a time, in relationship with Him. When we ask Him to begin the process of showing us what "perfect love" really feels like, the pleaser can begin to learn that she's only responsible for herself to God—she won't die if her spouse, her kids, or her friends fail, do the wrong thing, or if they become angry with her!

Reflection _____

Are you a people pleaser, or are you in a relationship with one?

Conversation with God _____

God, please give me an understanding of Your love, Your presence, and help me learn to live in Your peace, if I am a pleaser. Give me grace for those whom I love who struggle with pleasing.

---

22 Ibid.

Mirror Image
By Luisa Reyes-Ampil

Therefore be imitators of God, as beloved children.
And walk in love, as Christ loved us and gave himself
up for us, a fragrant offering and sacrifice to God.
EPHESIANS 5:1–2

It was late evening when I received a call from a new Filipina friend. Her husband had just physically abused her, and she didn't know where to go. I invited her to come to my house and stay until she could sort things out.

She was soon very comfortable. She would drive to my workplace for visits and would arrive wearing my clothes or my jewelry. That bothered me, but I thought I should be a blessing to her since she came only with an overnight bag.

When her divorce proceeding was in place, she eventually found a temporary job. Lo and behold, it was as an administrative assistant to the president at another Christian ministry—just like the job I held at the time. She would call me from time to time to get tips on how to do the job, and I felt like a mentor to her.

Since I was not able to host her any longer because I was in a rental home that didn't allow extended guest stays, my parents helped and took her in. It started getting weirder as she claimed to people that they were her parents. She was very sweet to them, but it began causing friction in our family as she was almost

70

taking over as their "daughter."

This budding friendship did not end well. After I confronted her on the problems that had developed, she literally ran away—like a small child. Owing me a substantial amount of money, she tried to use my home key—the one I had given her in the past—to return the money with just a note. Fortunately, we had changed our lock and key.

If you have seen thriller movies of someone imitating another person to a tee, you will understand that this situation was slowly moving in that direction as she attempted to become like me. I was hoping that she was attracted to me as a friend because of my Christian witness, learning from my own life journeys, and seeing Jesus in my life. But I should have known that there is only One we should imitate to mold us into better people, edging out the old sinful selves we have. His name? Jesus Christ. We are to follow in *His* footsteps in order to be transformed into the people God wants us to be.

I learned a hard lesson through this experience. Keep your eyes on the Lord—not others—for He will never disappoint you!

Reflection

Are you imitating Jesus as a child imitates his or her parent? It's the only reliable path to becoming a better you.

Conversation with God

I am excited for who I will become because of You!

Always Beautiful

By Darlene Sala

Behold, you are beautiful, my love.
SONG OF SOLOMON 4:1

Sometimes when you click on Facebook notifications on your phone or computer, you see a face you've never seen before—that is, until you glance at the name and realize it's someone you know well. The person has posted a new profile picture—and you didn't immediately recognize them. Chances are it's a girlfriend of yours who has taken a new selfie in a glamorous pose that she thinks makes her look prettier than the previous shot did. Come on, let's be honest: Who ever posts an ugly picture of herself on Facebook?

We all want to look as attractive as possible. The media and our culture contribute to this, continually tempting us to buy new clothes and more expensive makeup and to try a new hairstyle, thinking that all of these things will make us feel better about ourselves. And sometimes it works—for a while. But depending on these things for a sense of self-esteem can eventually lead us into a trap of superficiality and materialism.

Don't get me wrong. God loves beauty, and there's nothing wrong with wanting to look pretty. But beauty that is dependent on outward appearance alone is temporary at best.

In my book *Created for a Purpose*, I mention that we tend to get our sense of self-esteem from three sources:

* Our appearance
* Our abilities
* Our relationships

The problem with this is that all three of these sources can and will change during your lifetime. Aging will take its toll on your natural beauty. Someone will come along who can do your job better than you can. And even relationships will change as friends and relatives come and go in your life.

The only source of self-esteem that will never change is how God views us. He is the one who created our beauty, talents, and even relationships in the first place. He made us like He wants us, and His value of us never changes. He esteems us so highly that He gave His Son to pay the price for our sins so we could be forgiven and spend all eternity with Him.

Don't let the evil one get you on a detour in your relationship with God and your opinion of yourself. Keep your focus on Him and His view of your value. That viewpoint never changes.

Reflection

Your body is the frame God has chosen for the work of art He is creating in your life. Remember, the artist knows best which frame to choose.

Conversation with God

Keep my focus on You, Lord, so that Your beauty can be seen in my life.

Make It Personal

By Luisa Reyes-Ampil

The fear of the LORD is the beginning of wisdom,
and the knowledge of the Holy One is insight.
PROVERBS 9:10

I was raised in a Roman Catholic home, so my faith was something I was "born into" and "raised in." I got baptized, had my first confession, and received my first Holy Communion all on schedule. I learned Jesus Christ is the Son of God, who was born of the Virgin Mary, and that He died on the cross and rose again. But I just knew the facts of His birth, death, and resurrection, not the *real* story and that I can have a personal relationship with Him.

Jesus Christ decided to reveal Himself to me. First, I became involved in a Catholic Charismatic movement. I started reading the Bible—more like randomly flipping the pages with my finger pointing at my passage for the day.

Then I went through the Life in the Spirit and Growth in the Spirit seminars. I learned of the Holy Spirit and the spiritual gifts He can provide me. This time, I earnestly prayed to receive the specific gift that I wanted. But Proverbs 9:10 kept popping up: "The fear of the LORD is the beginning of wisdom, and the knowledge of the Holy One is insight." *No, Lord! I want one particular gift!*

Second, God started confronting me about many things

in my life, including my dying marriage. I traveled to the US with my children. And this time I seriously listened to the plan of salvation from my born-again Christian family instead of avoiding their attempts to share the Gospel with me. I didn't pray the "Sinner's Prayer," but I started reading the Bible more intentionally. I also decided to read commentaries to help me understand the Word better.

After God Himself revealed His truth to me, I had no more excuses to give, and I eventually said yes to Christ. *I had a choice in my faith this time!* And I could make my relationship with God as personal and as intimate as I wanted it to be!

I have seen the wonderful hand of God in my life. As I allowed my faith to grow, He put His perfect plan into motion and moved me to a richer relationship with Himself and others. I can sit back and enjoy the blessings of His love and grace in my life, remembering to pass it on to others.

Reflection

Is your faith in Christ so real and personal that you can stand on it no matter what happens?

Conversation with God

"Lead me to the rock that is higher than I" (Psalm 61:2).

Feeling Worthless
By Darlene Sala

"Are not two sparrows sold for a penny? And not one
of them will fall to the ground apart from your Father.
But even the hairs of your head are all numbered. Fear not,
therefore; you are of more value than many sparrows."
MATTHEW 10:29–31

I'm stunned by how much God loves us—no, actually I'm stunned
by how much God loves *me*, especially on those days when I
can't seem to do anything right and I feel so unlovable. Days
when I stay in my pajamas—all day. Times when I resent being
interrupted to help someone else. Evenings when I'm up too
late doing whatever on my laptop or phone.

Then I begin to think about how much God paid to have
a relationship with worthless-feeling me, and I am ashamed.
Ashamed that I've wasted the day that God gave me. Ashamed
that I've let my emotions run my life. Okay, so obviously, because
Jesus died for me, I'm not worthless, but equally obvious is that
I did not have my life under control today—or even my thoughts.

At the end of a bad day, when you finally collapse into bed,
do feelings of worthlessness wash over you? You lost your temper
when your son forgot his lunch for the second time this week.
After hurrying to get the laundry done, you found chewing gum
in the dryer (if you're blessed enough to have a dryer). At the
end of your day, your to-do list was even longer than when you

started the day. And you get no sympathy from your husband.

You feel utterly worthless and unlovable. But are you? If you think so, then Jesus died on the cross for nothing—a waste of divine suffering. When He died for you, He showed how much He loves you. He paid for your sins so you don't have to.

So, who are you going to believe? Your own depressing thoughts of worthlessness? Or what Jesus thinks of you?

The apostle John tells us, "See what kind of love the Father has given to us, that we should be called children of God; and so we are. . . . Beloved, we are God's children now, and what we will be has not yet appeared; but we know that when he appears we shall be like him, because we shall see him as he is" (1 John 3:1–2).

Okay, so you're not perfect now. But someday you will be! In the meantime, reject those thoughts of worthlessness and thank God that He wants to spend eternity with you.

Reflection

We can't stop thinking—but we can control what we think about.

Conversation with God

Remind me, God, that I can feel right about myself even on the days when I don't feel good about myself.

"I Solemnly Swear!"

By Luisa Reyes-Ampil

*But our citizenship is in heaven, and from
it we await a Savior, the Lord Jesus Christ.*
PHILIPPIANS 3:20

It was 1998, the year of big change. My nine-year-old twin daughters and I packed two suitcases each and moved from the Philippines to the US where I began work with Guidelines International Ministries. It would take three applications over a period of ten years to change our statuses from business professional and dependents to resident aliens to citizens!

When we went to the Los Angeles Convention Center for our oath-taking ceremony, we were joined by thousands more from all over the world. Together we pledged our allegiance to the United States and waved small American flags as we sang the national anthem. Eventually our brown Philippine passports were canceled, as we now proudly held blue US passports. I understand full well the implication of changing citizenship, for we gave up one life in exchange for another.

There was another change of citizenship that took place two years prior to that in my life. When I accepted Jesus Christ as my Lord and Savior, I had to surrender my old sinful nature so that I could become a new creation, a citizen of God's kingdom.

The application process for kingdom citizenship is very different from the earthly immigration process. First, there is no wait time. It doesn't take ten years to exchange your old life for new. It happens in an instant—at the moment you surrender your life to Christ. Second, there is no paperwork required. You only need to profess that you are a sinner, that you are turning control of your life over to Christ, and to ask Him to take charge. And last, you won't need to be fingerprinted—no background check required. In fact, criminals are welcome in the kingdom of God.

The benefits afforded me by my kingdom citizenship are unparalleled. First, I have hope no matter what I go through in life. Jesus Himself is my personal representative. Second, God is my host, and He promises to welcome me into eternal life when my time here in my earthly home is done.

Immigration in heaven will be very tight; IDs will be checked at the gate! "Nothing impure will ever enter it, nor will anyone who does what is shameful or deceitful," says Revelation 21:27 (NIV), "but only those whose names are written in the Lamb's book of life."

Reflection

Are you absolutely sure that your citizenship is in heaven, that your name is written in the "Lamb's book of life"? You can be.

Conversation with God

Lord, thank You for the opportunity to become a citizen of Your kingdom.

Desperate

By Darlene Sala

For we are his workmanship, created in Christ Jesus
for good works, which God prepared beforehand,
that we should walk in them.
EPHESIANS 2:10

She flipped over the page of the calendar. The new page—February—stared back at her, decorated with its lacy hearts and pink roses. Valentine's Day? Love? Even though she was still in her late teens, she could not relate. In her despair, instead of going downstairs for a drink, she turned to her computer to reach out to a voice she had heard on a Christian radio program: "Guidelines, a Five-Minute Commentary on Living."

> *It is the middle of the night, and here I am writing to you. I am supposed to be trusting in Jesus. But today I look to Him but I find no comfort. What is bothering me is me—who am I? I am only nineteen. My mother and father are gone. I am the last of nine children. I have two children I love, and they're all I have to live for. Please write me back.*

How could she be convinced God loved her? Not by her circumstances. She had hardly known love other than through her two children. Only one thing would be convincing enough to reach her in her misery: the truth that God loved her enough to sacrifice His Son, Jesus, for her. Love—real love that was costly, that wasn't dependent on her performance.

Are you in similar circumstances? Everyone in your life has disappointed you—you feel used up, and you're wondering who you are and why you are on the face of this earth. Let me assure you God does love you. He has a purpose for your life that will unfold as you walk with Him day by day. It won't always be easy, but as you hold on to Him in the hard times, you will find He will direct your life. As the writer of Psalm 57 said, "I cry out to God Most High, to God who fulfills his purpose for me" (v. 2).

Reflection

If you are at a point of desperation, don't give up! Fill your heart with the assurance that the God who died for you won't leave you now. He *will* fulfill His purpose for your life as you call out to Him.

Conversation with God

I do cry out to You, Lord. I'm desperate for You to show me You have a purpose for my life. I'm going to give each day to You and trust You to lead me in the way I should go.

He Knows My Frame
By Bonnie Sala

For He knows our frame;
He remembers that we are dust.
PSALM 103:14 NKJV

I love, love, love this verse! I love it because it is so encouraging to me on my journey into grace. My Father knows me. He keeps in mind that I'm. . .well, dust! He knows my anxious core, my unhealthy desire to please others rather than Him, and He knows how fear plays a faithless role in my life!

And I love the authenticity of God's Word because it tells me that other people—greats of the faith—have also had their "but dust" moments. Like Gideon. Gideon was one of the mightiest warriors in all of the Bible. And he was scared.

Judges 7 tells how God had given Gideon a mission, had hand-selected a fighting force for him and told him he was going to win! "Arise, go down against the camp, for I have given it into your hand," God said (v. 9). Here's the part I love: *"But if you are afraid to go down,* go down to the camp with Purah your servant. And you shall hear what they say, and afterward your hands shall be strengthened to go down against the camp" (vv. 10–11, emphasis added).

When Gideon and Purah snuck down to the outposts of the camp, they heard a man recounting a dream he had that foretold that Gideon and his three hundred men were going to decimate the enemies that were like "sand that is on the sea-shore in abundance" (v. 12). Gideon's response? "As soon as Gideon heard the telling of the dream and its interpretation, he worshiped" (v. 15).

God knew Gideon. He knew Gideon's "frame," his personality and his weaknesses. He knew that Gideon needed reassurance, and He not only allowed Gideon to see for himself how scared the enemy was but even sent Purah, Gideon's servant, with him on the spying mission the night before the battle. God knows that sometimes we need another human by our side.

God sees you today, in your weakness. It's okay with Him. He makes provision for it in the details of your life, if you have surrendered to Him.

Reflection

How has God met you, given you customized grace in your weakness? Do you need that grace today?

Conversation with God

I want to worship like Gideon did when he realized You were at work in his life! Thank You that You know me like no one else knows me. Thank You that You don't look down on me for my neediness. Thank You for remembering what I'm made of. Please provide what I need to walk through this day with You.

Me and Miss California

By Darlene Sala

*"Man looks on the outward appearance,
but the LORD looks on the heart."*

1 SAMUEL 16:7

One day my husband called me and said that Lisa needed a place to live for a few months, and asked what I thought of inviting her to live with us. Not one to wait for long periods of time before he makes a decision, my husband stayed on the phone for my answer.

You need to know something else about this decision. Lisa was beautiful—a two-time winner of the Miss California competition—part of the Miss America Pageant. Harold didn't know he had touched on an old insecurity of mine that cropped up whenever I was around beautiful women. The closest I ever came to being in a beauty pageant was being May Queen in kindergarten! Now the two of us were going to be living in the same house. I could just picture Lisa coming down the stairs for breakfast looking radiant while I was in my bathrobe looking like comedian Phyllis Diller. (Check the Internet to see the unique hairstyle she wore when playing a comedy role!)

What could I say? It would be very selfish of me to say no just because I had an insecurity that should have been dispatched long ago. We did have a spare bedroom available, so I couldn't use lack of space as an excuse. So with trepidation, I agreed that we would invite her to come. It was time for me to grow up.

You can probably guess that the ending to this story is a good one. Lisa proved to be beautiful not only on the outside but on the inside as well. She went on to help us on the Guidelines ministry television program and to become a close friend I love spending time with whenever possible.

How much I would have missed if I had listened to my insecurities instead of trusting that God knew what He was doing!

Reflection

"I thank God for protecting me from what I thought I wanted and blessing me with what I didn't know I needed." —Unknown.[23]

Conversation with God

Sometimes it's scary, Lord, when You ask me to do something outside my comfort zone. But I acknowledge that You know better than I do what I need. I'm going to trust one day at a time that You are sufficient for anything You ask me to do, starting today.

23 Pinterest, accessed October 31, 2016, https://www.pinterest.com/pin/138345019780478430/.

More Precious Than Diamonds

By Darlene Sala

"You are precious in my eyes. . .and I love you."
ISAIAH 43:4

I'm precious in God's eyes? Could it be true?

Think for a moment about diamonds. They are one of the most precious items in creation—rare, beautiful, and highly prized. But they are nothing compared to how God values us—we who trip and fall and fail more often than we care to admit.

If we're going to compare ourselves to diamonds, how much is a diamond worth anyway? In 2013, a nearly sixty-carat flawless pink diamond called the Pink Star was auctioned by Sotheby's for a whopping $83.2 million. Bling cha-ching! That made it the most expensive diamond ever sold at auction.

But the most precious diamond, we're told, is the Koh-i-noor, now part of the British crown jewels collection. Experts say this gem cannot be valued—it's calculated to be approximately 3.5 times the wealth of the whole world!

These diamonds are incredibly precious to us. But to God, diamonds just aren't that precious. Nor are other costly stones, or even gold. After all, in heaven He uses gold for paving streets, pearls for gates (Revelation 21:21), and gems to decorate the foundations of the heavenly city (Revelation 21:19).

But you? Now, that's another matter. God has formed many diamonds. But He made only one *you*. You are unique—unlike anyone else who has ever lived or ever will live, because He wants someone exactly like you. He has plans for you.

You may be feeling pretty worthless right now. You don't feel worth as much as a rhinestone, let alone a diamond. Take heart. "You are precious in my eyes," said God, "and I love you" (Isaiah 43:4). God never said He loved a diamond, but He does say He loves you.

Don't wait another minute. Run. Yes, run to His arms right now. Let Him whisper those words to you: "I love you. I love you." I think your heart will respond and say, "Lord, I love You, too!"

Reflection

What does it mean to *you* that God says, "*You are precious in my eyes, and I love you*"?

Conversation with God

God, I don't feel very lovable, no matter how hard I try, but today I'm going to assume You really mean it when You say that I am precious in Your sight, and You love me. I throw myself into Your arms. Thank You, thank You for a love that is bigger than all my mistakes.

Whitewashed

By Luisa Reyes-Ampil

*"In the same way, on the outside you appear
to people as righteous but on the inside you
are full of hypocrisy and wickedness."*
MATTHEW 23:28 NIV

I hate seeing a mess! I can't leave the office without making sure that my desk is all straightened up for the next day's work. I can't leave my house without making sure that my bed is made and the dirty dishes washed and set to dry. When I have a day off, I spend half of it cleaning our home—including bathing Newman, our terrier mix. You name it and I feel a need to clean it! My line of reasoning is this: what you present to the world should be what you are inside.

Is there any relationship between spiritual maturity and the physical state of my office or home? Perhaps not! But because I equate cleanliness outside to cleanliness inside, I tend to judge others the way I judge myself. The truth is, I have no business going around rating people's spiritual maturity based on their physical appearance. I am just making a judgment.

What we need to be sensitive to are those who appear to be righteous but are really sinful inside. They try to mislead people with their pretensions of spiritual maturity by going to church, keeping company with believers, and attending Bible studies. But in the secret of their homes, they have another side to them.

And in their hearts, they have motives that are not in line with God's Word. They think that they are bridging the gap between man and God with the godly way they act and talk, but they are only being deceptive.

It dawned on me that there are times we become legalistic or get stuck on appearances. "You are like whitewashed tombs, which look beautiful on the outside but on the inside are full of the bones of the dead and everything unclean," Jesus said to the Pharisees in Matthew 23:27 (NIV). "Hypocrites!" is Jesus' own word for them.

Do you have a beautiful home? Just make sure your home and your life are the same on the inside—a pleasing and holy sacrifice to Him for His purpose and will.

Reflection

What skeletons in the closet do you have that you need to get rid of?

Conversation with God

Lord, I want to be busy removing the clutter in my life and not just the physical mess in my home or workplace. I need to do away with my own pretensions and hypocrisies. Keep me clean and pleasing to You.

When People Stare at You
By Darlene Sala

*Not as though I had already attained, either were already
perfect: but I follow after, if that I may apprehend that
for which also I am apprehended of Christ Jesus.*
PHILIPPIANS 3:12 KJV

I was born with a dark port-wine birthmark on the left side of my face. I learned to get used to people staring and kids asking, "What's that on your face?" I admit this is a very minor defect to be concerned about. Many people have *major* birth defects that draw finger-pointing and unkind comments. But to me, as a kid, it was major.

Eventually, my mom learned about a cosmetic that would help conceal the birthmark. Life was better. But the color was not right for me and made me look as if I had hit the side of my face with a big white powder puff. I then got the comment, "Why do you have powder on your face?" Feeling different from everyone else in any way is debilitating! I just wanted to sink into a hole in the ground.

Yet, inside I had a great desire to make my life count for the Lord. I wanted to share the Word with others, not sit on the sidelines just because I felt insecure.

Then one Sunday morning my dad spoke on Philippians 3:12 (KJV): "I follow after, if that I may apprehend that for which also I am apprehended of Christ Jesus." He explained that *apprehend* meant "to lay hold of." The truth dawned in my heart:

* God has laid hold of me for a purpose—*His* purpose.
* God's purpose is unique. I don't have to be like anyone else. I just have to be me—imperfect but unique me. The thought still brings tears to my eyes because it was so freeing.

Philippians 3:12 became my life verse. Whenever I feel insecurity coming back to defeat me, I realize His purpose for me is not the same as His purpose for you. I can admire the beauty in your life and ask God to make that a reality in my life. But that's up to the Holy Spirit to accomplish, not something I should try to achieve on my own.

In the years that followed I had a series of laser surgeries that removed most of the birthmark. Add a bit of concealer, and—*voilà*—the birthmark is no longer a problem.

Reflection
"But he said to me, 'My grace is sufficient for you, for my power is made perfect in weakness'" (2 Corinthians 12:9).

Conversation with God
Thank You, Lord, that we don't have to be perfect for You to use us for Your glory. In spite of imperfections we can be a blessing serving You.

He Is for Me!

By Bonnie Sala

What shall we say about such wonderful things as these?
If God is for us, who can ever be against us?
ROMANS 8:31 NLT

I was out walking my dogs, earphones in with my praise music going, when the words of the song I was listening to suddenly struck me: *"He is for me, He is not against me."*

It was one of those strange moments when I realized I had forgotten something really important about God. Growing up as the eldest child in a Christian home, it was far too easy to slip into wanting to please—first my parents, then teachers, employers, and yes, God. Faith as a checklist of things to do and *not* do, instead of a real *relationship* with Jesus.

But by the time you've got a few years on you, something inside of you knows that you've blown it many, many a time, and then you're really not sure that Jesus is indeed standing and knocking at the door of your heart saying, "If you hear my voice and open the door, I will come in, and we will share a meal together as friends" (Revelation 3:20 NLT). I think I had started to subconsciously believe He'd be standing there like a supervisor, with checklist and clipboard, saying, "So, let's discuss a few things. . . ."

Of course, this is the work of Satan, the accuser. Do you remember what John says? "If anyone does sin, we have an advocate who pleads our case before the Father" (1 John 2:1 NLT). Jesus. Standing next to me, in front of God the Father, making the case for my forgiveness, my justification. And that brings me a flood of relief. I remember now, He loves me intimately. Jesus says, "See, I have written your name on the palms of my hands" (Isaiah 49:16 NLT).

Reflection

Do you live your life fearlessly, like you really *believe* that God is *for you*?

Conversation with God

Father, help me with any unbelief. Let me learn to rest in Your love, Your favor. Thank You for accepting me, forgiving me, and for working out Your very best in my life at all times!

A Lifestyle of Service
By Luisa Reyes-Ampil

For you were called to freedom, brothers.
Only do not use your freedom as an opportunity
for the flesh, but through love serve one another.
GALATIANS 5:13

Some of the popular Disney princesses didn't exactly have lives of ease—not until their Prince Charmings arrived to rescue them. Banished Princess Snow White had to live with the seven dwarfs and waited on them in exchange for a roof over her head. After her wealthy father died, Cinderella had to do the house chores from morning until night for her stepmother and stepsisters, falling asleep, tired to the bone. And Sleeping Beauty had to say good-bye to her castle, to grow up in a simple cottage with her godmothers. She had to do the occasional sweeping. But our princesses demonstrated lives of service!

I have to admit, it's nice to wake up to your breakfast even if it's not in bed. It's even better to come home to a hot dinner no matter how late you are. It's great to be driven around by a driver, without worries over parking and walking in the heat or rain. I grew up in a country where house help made these luxuries a reality—our maids and driver made sure they served our needs every single day no matter what time of day when we lived in Manila. When I talk about my past life to my American friends, it almost sounds like a fairy tale to them. But Jesus just had to shake me and my very comfortable life!

Galatians 5:13 says, "For you were called to freedom, brothers. Only do not use your freedom as an opportunity for the flesh, but through love serve one another." One by one, Jesus peeled away my dependence on others. I learned how to cook and clean the house. I learned how to do laundry. I learned how to pump gas at the station. I eventually raised my kids without help from nannies (seldom done in the culture of my birth).

A lifestyle of service was demonstrated daily for me for more than thirty years, and I am forever grateful for the privilege. Today, however, God continues to challenge me to a lifestyle of service for others. God showed me how He loves me and how I can love others so I can be equipped to serve wherever He takes me. It's my new lifestyle of service!

Reflection

What kind of lifestyle are you living right now? Does it conflict with God's call to a lifestyle of service for Him?

Conversation with God

Thank You, Lord, for teaching me to value the service of others in my lifetime. I pray that I will honor You as I serve others.

Forgiveness: Traveling Light

How and why you can let it go

Excusing or Forgiving?
By Darlene Sala

As the Lord has forgiven you, so you also must forgive.
COLOSSIANS 3:13

My friend Dr. Richard Smith tells of counseling a woman who had been gang-raped as a teen. Although she was a believer and said she had forgiven the men, years later the trauma still haunted her.

"On what grounds did you forgive the men who raped you?" Richard asked her.

"On the same grounds," she replied, "that Christ did. 'Father, forgive them, for they know not what they do.'"

Richard writes, "What [she] did sounds nice and spiritual, even pious, but it is not forgiveness by God's standard. [Forgiveness] means that we hold people accountable for their deeds, without excuse. We fully understand the awfulness of what they have done and then we forgive and extend mercy."

Then he writes something that we often forget: "Even when we fully understand what they have done, God would have us forgive—not excuse. How do we excuse?" Richard lists phrases that we often use: "*They are just human. They did the best they could. They did not know what they were doing. They lost control. They grew up in a terrible home.*"

While these phrases possibly explain their behavior, there can be no excuse for sin, not from God's point of view or from ours. The sinner deserves to pay for what he or she did. We are commanded to forgive, not because it doesn't matter, but because God will see that justice is done on our behalf.

Richard explains that "when we forgive, we are giving that other person over into God's hands and taking our hands off, trusting that God will see that justice is done. He will see that a payment for sin is made—either by that person or by Christ,"[24] who died for all of our sins on the cross.

Where are you in this process of forgiveness? Is your heart still full of anger and rage at what was done to you? Or can you put the matter in God's hands to see that justice is done on your behalf?

Reflection

You know you have truly forgiven someone when you are willing for God to extend mercy to the one who wronged you, if that's what He chooses.

Conversation with God

Dear Lord, with all my heart I forgive that person who You know wronged me. I put them in Your hands to judge—to punish or to show mercy. I realize I have no right to refuse to forgive when You have forgiven me.

---

24 Dr. Richard Smith, "Forgiveness: Fact & Fiction," *Insights* (Bland, VA: Cross Ministries, n.d.).

Bypassing Bitterness
By Bonnie Sala

---

*Therefore do not pronounce judgment before the time, before
the Lord comes, who will bring to light the things now hidden
in darkness and will disclose the purposes of the heart.
Then each one will receive his commendation from God.*

1 CORINTHIANS 4:5

"I have a question," the e-mail read. "How can I forgive people who insulted me, lied to me, and humiliated me for a long time? It was a very difficult time for me, but I could not change the situation. Now I have escaped from this hell but I have a strong desire for revenge. I want them to feel what I felt when they jeered at me."

I empathize with this woman who was now physically free and yet trapped with her pain in a different prison: the prison of bitterness. I understood her feelings though, for I, too, had been betrayed and mistreated. What was done to us was wrong; our pain is real and our perpetrators' actions were sinful. Two facts were helpful to me in escaping the chains of bitterness.

You and I do not have the *authority* to mete out the punishment a wrongdoer deserves. Remember that God says, "Vengeance is *mine*" (Romans 12:19, emphasis added)? Vengeance actually belongs to God. Author Lou Priolo says when we impatiently try to avenge ourselves, it's like walking up to God and taking His crown off His head! It shows a very poor understanding of who God is and what He is about. It says, "God, I don't trust You to be just."

We also don't have the *ability* to do the job that needs to be done. We don't have all of the facts. "Suppose," says Priolo, "he has done the same thing to twelve other people this month and deserves a more serious judgment than you would think to give him. The amount of vengeance required by God's justice is predicated on His knowledge of men's motives."[25] "I will repay," says the Lord. If you doubt God's ability to take care of your enemies, just do a little reading in the Old Testament! God is serious about sin—it cost Him His only Son's life, and His justice is the only perfect justice that exists.

Reflection

Is there anyone in your past or in your life today that you wish you could get back at?

Conversation with God

God, please forgive me if I've tried to take things into my own hands when I've been wronged. Thank You that I can rest on the promise that You will dispense Your perfect justice in Your perfect time.

---

25 Lou Priolo, *Bitterness* (Phillipsburg, NJ: P&R Publishing, 2008), 32.

No More Condemnation

By Darlene Sala

There is therefore now no condemnation
for those who are in Christ Jesus.

ROMANS 8:1

A friend of mine wrote me about the guilt she was experiencing:

Condemnation—I felt it every day. The enemy would
whisper—no, actually more like scream—denunciation
into my ear for the daily sins I was committing.

Please understand that this was not conviction. This
was a feeling of condemnation, a feeling that I was a bad
person, a feeling that I was not worthy of being a child of
God. These feelings stirred up fear in me that I was going
to hell. I found myself being condemned all the time about
daily sins. And I mean—all the time. How was I ever going
to make it to heaven if I couldn't live a sinless life?

I am driving on the highway, and I can't stay under
the speed limit. Oh, I tried, because if I hit one mile over,
I was breaking the law and that was sin. If I clicked the
AGREE button at the beginning process of downloading
something on my computer, stating that I accept the
terms and conditions, but I actually had not read the
entire document, I lied. In my mind, I needed to be
perfect. But how could I?

Here's my question for you: If every little thing we do wrong is a sin, and there's no sin in heaven, how are any of us going to make it there?

The good news is that no matter the size of our sinning, there's a solution: God forgives us because Jesus paid for all our sins when He died on the cross. He didn't die only for big sins; He died for all our sins. "For all have sinned and fall short of the glory of God, and are justified by his grace as a gift, through the redemption that is in Christ Jesus" (Romans 3:23–24).

Yes, we have the problem of needing daily forgiveness for sins of all sizes. The Bible tells us that "if we say we have no sin, we deceive ourselves" (1 John 1:8). But the very next verse says, "If we confess our sins, he is faithful and just to forgive us our sins and to cleanse us from all unrighteousness." No limits. No expiration date.

No, we don't want to sin intentionally. When we do, however, forgiveness is available from a loving heavenly Father.

Reflection

"In [Jesus] we have redemption through his blood, the forgiveness of our trespasses, according to the riches of his grace, which he lavished upon us" (Ephesians 1:7–8).

Conversation with God

Dear Lord, thank You for paying the price to forgive my sins—big and little.

Choosing to Be a Peacemaker
By Luisa Reyes-Ampil

*"But if you do not forgive others their trespasses,
neither will your Father forgive your trespasses."*
MATTHEW 6:15

In the aftermath of a broken marriage, there are critical choices to be made. I chose the role of a peacemaker not just for my children's sake but also for my spiritual well-being—I was a new Christian, but I wanted to live by the principles I was learning in the Bible.

" 'But if you do not forgive others their trespasses, neither will your Father forgive your trespasses' " (Matthew 6:15) stood out to me during my legal hearings and custody battle. It shone like a beacon for me when my children and I moved from the Philippines to the US, and I wanted to keep the lines of communication open.

Some thought that I was trying to keep the "love flame" burning in the hope of reconciliation with my ex-husband. Honestly, it was all about helping rebuild the broken relationship between the girls, who were so young when it all happened, and their father and his family. For many years, I bought, wrote, and mailed the Christmas cards and enclosed the girls' most current photos, calling their paternal grandparents on special occasions. But I found my children disconnected and short on words during the calls. My children wondered why I wanted to give their distant grandparents updates.

When my children turned eighteen, I decided my peace-making job was done. As adults, they can take care of their own family business—that is, if they, too, choose to forgive.

A few years ago now, my ex-father-in-law became very ill, and I received a message that he was in the hospital. I was asked to rally in prayer! I went one step further and called my ex-husband, who happened to be at the hospital. His father wanted to speak with me after hearing I was on the line. "Thank you for taking the burden of caring for the girls all these years! I love you and I want you to tell the girls that I love them very much." A day or two later, he passed away.

The words of gratitude wouldn't have been said if not for peacemaking efforts on my part. But I also knew that I couldn't have been a peacemaker if I didn't ask the Lord to help me forgive my ex-husband. This business of forgiveness is hard as you strip yourself of pride, but not impossible with God!

Reflection

Have you made any efforts toward forgiveness of a wrongdoing done by someone you love or loved?

Conversation with God

Help me, Father, to see my role and responsibility in making things right.

The Journey of Forgiveness
By Bonnie Sala

Forgiving one another, as God in Christ forgave you.
EPHESIANS 4:32

It's a subject that makes us all uncomfortable. We *know* we are to forgive those who have hurt us. "But it was *wrong*," we cry out! We feel that there is no way to move past the pain, the injustice. "Forgiveness," wrote Ray Pritchard, "is not so much an event as it is an ongoing condition of the heart. It's a journey, not a destination. No one makes that journey easily or quickly. And no one makes that journey without God."[26]

The old saying was right: to err is human, to forgive divine. We are commanded to forgive as Christ forgave us, and here we confront a paradox: "We are commanded to do that which only God can do for us. If God does not do it for us, we will never do it on our own."

* Forgiveness isn't about you or the person who hurt you so deeply.

* Forgiveness is about God.

* We forgive because God has forgiven us and has commanded us to forgive.

---

26 Ray Pritchard, *The Healing Power of Forgiveness* (Eugene, OR: Harvest House, 2005), 8.

✱ We forgive because God has given us the strength to forgive.[27]

When we think of forgiveness, we need to think of the cross and what happened there. We had a death sentence on our heads that we were not going to escape; we were not going to be forgiven by God. But because Jesus *chose to die*, we were released from our own death sentences. His sacrificial death made all the forgiving that would ever be done possible, which is why we remember—" 'Do this in remembrance of me' " (1 Corinthians 11:24). We remember that the strength for our journey of forgiveness comes from the cross.

Jesus started all the forgiving right there on the cross. "Father, forgive them; for they know not what they do" (Luke 23:34 KJV). The crowd didn't even ask for forgiveness. They didn't repent. They jeered, "You saved others; save yourself" (see Matthew 27:42). And Jesus asked the Father for the first act of forgiveness in the history of humankind. When you think of the cross, remember that it is a promise of the power to forgive.

Reflection

Are you traveling a journey of forgiveness in your life today?

Conversation with God

God, I want to forgive because You've forgiven me. I surrender my pain to You and ask You to empower me to deliver the wrongdoer in my life to You and to forgive.

27 Ibid., 9.

As We Have Forgiven
By Luisa Reyes-Ampil

*"And forgive us our sins, as we have
forgiven those who sin against us."*
MATTHEW 6:12 NLT

Growing up in a poor family in Cebu, Philippines, Genalyn recalled how her parents always worked hard to provide for her and her five brothers. As she was the only daughter, her parents were very strict and made sure that she only went to school and came home on time each day.

By the time she turned nineteen, Genalyn's mother brought her to a mail-order bride agency, for her mom's dream was to marry her to a foreigner. Her name was eventually published in a pen-pal column of a newspaper, and her photo was also sent to an uncle serving in the US Navy to "shop around" to his friends.

Frank, a divorced middle-aged father and serviceman, soon started a correspondence. Genalyn, however, was not interested, but her mother forced her to sit down and respond to his letters. Mother also made sure to mail them. This went on for six months.

"I cannot see myself married to him!" was Genalyn's cry when Frank came to the Philippines to meet her and her family. She refused the special immigration papers for fiancées that Frank brought for her. Chastised for being prideful and disobedient, Genalyn's mom even suggested that she would die of heartache if Genalyn refused Frank. Genalyn soon found herself signing the papers and traveling to the United States—thousands of miles away from her family to a land where she didn't know anyone.

Four years of marriage and one child later, Genalyn's loveless marriage crumbled. Frank, who was retired by then and without any drive to seek a job to support his family, lost their home. They were soon sleeping on the floors of other people's homes.

Although Genalyn walked away from the Lord because of her circumstances, she eventually found her way back. Growing up in a Christian home, she had known that only God could fill the empty void in her. Genalyn returned to His unconditional love, but more amazingly, she learned to forgive her family for the betrayal she felt.

We often suffer for the mistakes of others. God's work in our lives is never limited by the circumstances of our lives or even the mistakes of others! He always makes a way possible for us to forgive.

Reflection

Are there those in your life whom you need to forgive for causing you harm?

Conversation with God

Thank You that no one can stop Your work in my life and that You make forgiveness possible.

Running to Us with Forgiveness

By Darlene Sala

" 'Let us eat and celebrate. For this my son was dead,
and is alive again; he was lost, and is found.' "

LUKE 15:23–24

If you want to understand what grace is, take another look at the story of the prodigal son found in Luke 15—the familiar account of the son who asks his father for his share of the inheritance, goes off and wastes it all, and ends up penniless and hungry. Eventually he decides to go home to his father, hoping that he can get a job as a hired servant.

In the Middle Eastern church the story goes by another name: The Story of the Running Father.[28] And that title changes the whole focus of the story from the failing son to the forgiving father.

The father sees his son a long way off and runs to him, something not usually done by Middle Eastern men. In a Proverbs 31 Ministries blog, Sherri Gragg points out that

running required men to hike up their robes and expose
their legs, which was considered humiliating and
disgraceful. The reason he was running was even more

28 Sherri Gragg, "*The Story of the Running Father*," Proverbs 31 Ministries, May 27, 2014, accessed April 3, 2017, http://proverbs31.org/devotions/devo/the-story-of-the-running-father/.

significant. It was a very serious matter for a Jewish young man to lose his family's inheritance in a foreign land. If he did, and he had the gall to actually return to his village, his entire community would then bring him to justice through a custom called the Kezazah. Once the community discovered the money was lost, they would surround him and break a pot at his feet. Then they would announce that from that moment on he was cut off from his family and community...as if he were dead.[29]

But this father had been watching—and hoping—for his son's return. So when he saw him, he did what no respected Middle Eastern man would do: he hiked up his robe and ran to him. And before the boy could give the speech he had prepared, the father embraced him and called for a banquet in his honor.

This, Jesus tells us, is what God is like. Not a cold, callous judge, but a father running—yes, running toward us to offer forgiveness and restoration.

Reflection

What a picture of grace—God's unmerited favor—toward us!

Conversation with God

Sometimes when I've blown it, God, I'm so hesitant to come to You. Thank You for reminding me that You've been watching for me to come back. You will run to meet me, forgive me, and assure me of Your grace and love.

29 Ibid.

Piecing Together Broken Hearts
By Luisa Reyes-Ampil

*Let all bitterness and wrath and anger and clamor
and slander be put away from you, along with all
malice. Be kind to one another, tenderhearted,
forgiving one another, as God in Christ forgave you.*
EPHESIANS 4:31–32

My very first encounter with brokenness was at the age of seventeen. Our mom and youngest sister went for a vacation and never returned. Along with two more siblings, we were suddenly left with our dad in the Philippines, with our "missing" mom and sister in the United States. What happened to our family? We had no inkling what went wrong because we had never heard our parents fight.

We all struggled emotionally, with our dad affected the most. He was suddenly a single parent to two college-aged young women and one high schooler. And because he was afraid to lose more of his children, he became even more protective. Our curfew was changed from midnight to 11 p.m.; sometimes we were not even allowed to leave the home except to go to school.

So instead of focusing on the pain, my siblings and I decided to protect each other and to rise above the brokenness. We put our hearts and minds into our studies and finished our degrees. We wanted to make sure that our parents would not experience any heartache because of wrong choices on our part. We all coped with our changed family life the best we could.

The brokenness between our parents continued and affected not only their children but their grandkids as well over the years. Eventually our dad remarried. We had a difficult time when both sets of parents were around, and never got to celebrate special occasions such as graduations or child dedications as a family. We divided ourselves between our parents so that neither would feel left out. That, of course, caused us a lot of stress and hard feelings over the years.

God put His restoration plan to work in a strange play of events. Our dad and his wife were arriving in the US for a visit when our stepdad died from an accidental fall. Although we were grieving, the Lord turned everything to a beautiful beginning of forgiveness and healing as our dad and his wife stepped in and spent time helping care for some of our mom's needs.

Reflection

Will you make the choice to forgive someone for your sake and others?

Conversation with God

Lord, help me to bring peace, even if I have to be the first to take the step toward forgiveness.

Hope for the Journey

"And you will feel secure, because there is hope" (Job 11:18).

Hope for the Journey
By Bonnie Sala

We have this as a sure and steadfast anchor of the soul,
a hope that enters into the inner place behind the curtain.
HEBREWS 6:19

"We are terrible *hopers* in this day and age," says Francis Chan. "We expect the worst because we've been let down too much. If something even halfway decent happens in a day we consider that a good day."[30] The Bible says that "hope deferred makes the heart sick" (Proverbs 13:12). Perhaps you feel that there isn't much hope on your journey through this life.

The truth is, the here and now, our bank accounts, our accomplishments, anything that we can touch, see, and feel, even the people around us that we love best, were never meant to give us hope. They were never designed to lead to what the Bible calls the "hope [that] does not disappoint" (Romans 5:5 NKJV). Paul laid it out straight for us: "Through him we have also obtained access by faith into this grace in which we stand, and we rejoice in *hope of the glory of God*" (Romans 5:2, emphasis added). The problem is, Chan says, "Hope in the glory of God doesn't anchor our souls!"[31]

Hope in God's glory won't do us any good if God's glory is little more than a nice-sounding religious sentiment. The

---

30 Francis Chan (address, Finishing the Task conference, Lake Forest, CA, December 2016).
31 Ibid.

glory of God is in the Gospel: God's story of Jesus' death for us, resurrection, and our redemption and restoration back into right relationship with Him. "When the story is told and the gospel is preached, what shines out from it, Paul says in 2 Corinthians 4:4, is 'the light of the gospel of the glory of Christ, who is the image of God.' "[32]

Is your heart sick? Has your journey been marked by potholes of disappointment? Maybe we've all lost sight of His glory because we've lost sight of our need for the Gospel. Maybe we've lost sight of His glory because listening to Him and reading His love story has been relegated to the leftover time in our lives. "Are you *thrilled with Him* right now?"[33] Chan challenges us.

Reflection

What gives you hope?

Conversation with God

Father, please open the eyes of my heart; help me get my eyes off myself, off the here and now, and to see the glory of the Gospel!

---

32 John Piper, "Let Us Exult in the Glory of God!" Desiring God, October 24, 1999, accessed December 13, 2016, http://www.desiringgod.org/messages/let-us-exult-in-the-hope-of-the-glory-of-god.

33 Chan, address at Finishing the Task conference.

Someone Is Expecting Me

By Darlene Sala

*For the Lord himself will come down from heaven with
a commanding shout.... First, the believers who have
died will rise from their graves. Then, together with them,
we who are still alive and remain on the earth will be caught
up in the clouds to meet the Lord in the air. Then we will be
with the Lord forever. So encourage each other with these words.*
1 THESSALONIANS 4:16–18 NLT

Back in 2008, because of the global financial crisis, the Baikalsk
Pulp & Paper Mill, located in the wasteland of Siberia, shut down.
Now, for most towns, this would create a serious problem for
those who worked at the mill. For this little town it was a full-
blown crisis, for the mill was the primary source of jobs for the
seventeen thousand people who lived there. When the mill shut
down, other businesses folded. People went into survival mode,
unscrewing all but one lightbulb in their homes to save money
on electricity. They stayed in bed in the mornings because there
was nothing to get up for. Alcohol consumption rose.

Could they have moved to another area and looked for
work? Yes, but the idea of moving from remote Baikalsk was
scary for most of these people because they had never lived
in any other part of Russia. Their fathers had built the plant,
and many, after having been born in Baikalsk and growing up
there, had met their mate while working at the plant and put

down roots. In an interview, Svetlana Brovkin put it like this: "There's no place for us to go," she says. "Nobody's waiting for us. Nobody's expecting us."[34] What a sad, sad situation! No place to go. Nobody waiting, nobody expecting you.

Contrast this with the words of Jesus just before He died on the cross: "My Father's house has many rooms. . .I am going there to prepare a place for you. And if I go and prepare a place for you, I will come back and take you to be with me that you also may be where I am" (John 14:2–3 NIV).

Yes, we have a place to go, someone waiting for us, someone expecting us. Jesus has promised to come back to this earth and take us to be with Him. What's more, He tells us He's bringing with him those believers who have died already—a grand reunion. Together forever. What a day!

Reflection

We're never ever abandoned, never forsaken, never alone—no matter what changes life brings.

Conversation with God

Thank You, Lord, that You're preparing a place for me to be with You for all eternity.

---

34 Megan K. Stack, "Pulp Mill's Closure Puts a Russian Town in Peril," *Los Angeles Times*, December 21, 2008, accessed August 2, 2016, http://articles.latimes.com/2008/dec/21/world/fg-mill21/2.

Lesson from a Squirrel

By Luisa Reyes-Ampil

"Therefore I tell you, do not be anxious about your life, what you will eat or what you will drink. . . . Is not life more than food?"

MATTHEW 6:25

I was sitting in my fiancé Ken's family room looking out at the garden where a bird feeder hangs. A squirrel was slowly making its way to it for its morning feast. It looked to be dangling dangerously with its hind legs wrapped around the feeder while quickly grabbing a handful of the seeds with its front paws. This scene lasted for more than thirty minutes.

As Ken and I sat drinking our coffee, fascinated by the squirrel, I thought of Matthew 6 and our anxiety over our daily life of strife. Yes, we all understand the human necessity of needing to work to put food on the table, clothes on our backs, and so forth. Many of us are stuck in the rat race, running around, some with two jobs or more, so we can pay the mortgage or rent, buy gas for the cars, help send the kids to college, and the list goes on.

But God says, "Stop! Do not be anxious about your life!" *What?* Yes, our Lord is telling us that we are living under an open heaven and He has created everything for us to enjoy. All we need is to sit back and take what He offers us by faith. Whoa! We still don't get it!

I asked Ken why he refills the bird feeder the moment it's out of seeds. He doesn't need to do this, because the birds and the squirrel could just scavenge for food wherever. But Ken simply enjoys having the birds—and the squirrel—come around every day and take their fill of the feast. He takes pleasure in buying the feed and providing for them.

That's exactly what God is saying! God knows what we need for the day, and all we need is to allow Him to do His work so we can see Him as our Great Provider. He takes pleasure in meeting our needs.

Reflection

What lesson can you learn from the squirrel and the "birds of the air"?

Conversation with God

Thank You, Lord, that You are concerned with our daily needs and You want to provide for us. Help us not to be so anxious as we struggle with our jobs and other means of livelihood but instead to trust and obey. Then we will be blessed by Your giving hands and heart.

Jeremiah's Secret

By Bonnie Sala

"When I discovered your words, I devoured them.
They are my joy and my heart's delight, for I bear
your name, O LORD God of Heaven's Armies."
JEREMIAH 15:16 NLT

Jeremiah had a terrible life. God had set him apart before he was even born to be a prophet to the nations (Jeremiah 1:5). Called the "Weeping Prophet," Jeremiah's whole career centered around one purpose: delivering really bad news. Not only had the people of Judah exchanged the Lord for worthless idols, but they were sacrificing their children to them by throwing them into the fires of Molech (Jeremiah 32:35).

On his journey of deprivation and continual rejection, Jeremiah bore the sad burden of knowing in advance that God's disobedient people weren't going to listen and also knowing what was going to happen to them. He bore this burden alone, for God told him not to marry or have children (Jeremiah 16:2) because times were so awful. Jeremiah was much like the single mom who teaches her children in the way of the Lord, only to watch them choose to go their own way—and she can do little more than sit and wait for the coming train wreck.

How did Jeremiah do it? The answer is that "Jeremiah woke up each day and greeted it as a day *with and for* the Lord."[35] That's

---

35 Heald, *A Woman's Journey*, 103.

it. No matter what that day held, good or bad (and in Jerry's case they were pretty much all bad), if the day began with God, the day was a success.

The secret of his longevity was to be found in Jeremiah's "purpose-driven life." "Jeremiah did not resolve to stick it out for twenty-three years no matter what; he got up every morning with the sun. The day was God's day, not the people's. He didn't get up to meet with rejection, he got up to meet with God. He didn't rise to put up with another round of mockery, he rose to be with his Lord. That is the secret of his persevering pilgrimage."[36]

The same Word that sustained Jeremiah in the worst of times will also enable us to persevere on the journeys our loving Father has apportioned for us.

Reflection ⎯⎯⎯⎯⎯⎯⎯⎯⎯⎯⎯⎯⎯⎯⎯⎯⎯⎯

What would your level of satisfaction in life be if your sole purpose was to connect with God each day?

Conversation with God ⎯⎯⎯⎯⎯⎯⎯⎯⎯⎯⎯⎯⎯⎯

Father, please give me Your Word for me today; I look to You alone.

---

36 Ibid.

Graduation Day

By Darlene Sala

*Our Lord Jesus Christ. . .died for us so that whether we
are awake or asleep we might live with him. Therefore
encourage one another and build one another up.*
1 THESSALONIANS 5:9–11

I was always quite close to my uncle Phil, so when he passed
away, I grieved deeply. I would miss him very much—I still do.
He and his wife, Margaret, were a strong Christian influence in
my life, especially during the teen years.

A few days after he was gone, a longtime mutual friend, Dr.
Dorothy Jean Furlong, wrote these words to me: "Don't think I'm
hard-hearted, but I think sometimes believers need to remember
Paul's words 'to die is gain.' " She was referring to a verse in the
first chapter of the apostle Paul's letter to the Philippians that
says, "For to me to live is Christ, and to die is gain" (v. 21). The
New Living Translation puts it this way: "For to me, living means
living for Christ, and dying is even better," for it's our graduation day.

I realized she is right. When you know the Lord, to die *is* an
improvement. Now, don't misunderstand; it's normal to grieve
when a friend or family member dies. When Lazarus died, Jesus
wept. But for the person who has a personal relationship with
Jesus Christ, death is the friend who ushers him into the presence
of his Savior at the end of life. In heaven he will forever be free

from pain and suffering. No more tears, no more sorrow—only the joy of being with Jesus and all his friends and loved ones who have gone ahead of him into the presence of the Lord.

The prophet Isaiah said that instead of sorrow and sighing, we'll experience gladness and joy. He wrote that the ransomed of the Lord "will enter Zion with singing; everlasting joy will crown their heads. Gladness and joy will overtake them, and sorrow and sighing will flee away" (Isaiah 35:10 NIV).

That sounds to me like a pretty good trade-off for the problems, illness, heartache, and grief that we experience here on earth. These are encouraging words as we progress on this journey into grace.

Reflection

Perhaps today you can encourage someone else with these words—or if he or she is not a believer, share the good news that we can put our faith in Jesus and then live with joy for what is ahead.

Conversation with God

Thank You, Lord, that I don't have to dread the future. Someday all the pain of this life will be over and I'll spend eternity with You. In the meantime, help me learn how to use every moment for You.

Head in the Sand, Heart in His Hand

By Bonnie Sala

When I am afraid, I put my trust in you.
PSALM 56:3

Learning to trust God is a habit that I will be working on from now until eternity. For the first half of my adult life, I don't think I really had any idea what trusting God was actually all about. Oh, I prayed about things. I could quote Bible verses about faith. David may have been able to say, "When I am afraid, I put my trust in you," but I would have had to say, "When I am afraid. . . well. . .*I'm just really afraid!*"

What was I really trusting in? My own best efforts? My plans? My "control freak" attention to detail? God had to circle me in, to reduce my options through the circumstances He allowed in my life, to bring me to the place where I had nothing left to lean on. Except God. Yep, it came down to that. The Creator of heaven and earth.

When I tried taking my first baby steps of faith, my flesh told me, "This is a terrible idea—this is so irresponsible!" There I was, *just doing nothing* but praying and looking to God with my problems! It felt like I was putting my head down in the sand and hoping it would all work out!

"May the God of hope fill you with all joy and peace as you *trust* in him, so that you may overflow with *hope* by the power of the Holy Spirit," I read in Romans 15:13 (NIV, emphasis added).

"Holy Spirit," I wrote in my journal, "I can do this by Your power. I cannot trust apart from You. I need to overflow with hope for my family's sake!" To be sure, it was a fragile trust at first, but as Calvin Miller wrote, "Fragile trust is stronger than swaggering self-reliance."[37]

And slowly God worked in me. I had to ask myself, was I willing to accept circumstances as from His hand and accept them with gratitude, as the cup He was offering? Or would I continue to charge Him, as Elisabeth Elliot used to say, with "a mistake in His measurements, with misjudging the sphere in which I [could] best learn to trust Him"?[38]

Reflection _____

Do you struggle to trust God with your problems?

Conversation with God _____

Teach me, Father, to trust You. I am willing to be made willing to accept all that comes to me as from Your hand.

---

37 Calvin Miller, "Random Quotes, Helpful Thoughts," Journal of a Journey, December 11, 2007, accessed December 16, 2016, http://myjournalofajourney.blogspot .com/2007/12/random-quotes-helpful-thoughts.html.

38 Elisabeth Elliot, *Keep a Quiet Heart* (Grand Rapids, MI: Revell, 2004), quoted in "Elisabeth Elliot: A Quiet Heart," Stray Thoughts, September 18, 2008, accessed December 16, 2016, https://barbarah.wordpress.com/2008/09/18/elisabeth-elliot-a-quiet-heart/.

When the Hawks Are Circling

By Darlene Sala

He will cover you with his feathers,
and under his wings you will find refuge.
PSALM 91:4 NIV

Peggy Joyce Ruth stood observing their old mother hen and her brood of chickens that were scattered all over the yard. As she watched, she began to notice the shadow of a hawk that was circling overhead. The drama played out before her:

> *That mother hen did not run to those little chicks and jump on top of them to try to cover them with her wings. No! Instead, she squatted down, spread out her wings and began to cluck. And those little chickens, from every direction, came running to her to get under those outstretched wings. Then the hen pulled her wings down tight, tucking every little chick safely under her. To get to those babies, the hawk would have to go through the mother.*[39]

Psalm 91:4 (NIV) immediately came to her mind: "[God] will cover you with his feathers, and under his wings you will find

---

39 Peggy Joyce Ruth, "Lessons from a Chicken," *Charisma Home*, July 7, 2010, accessed March 8, 2015, http://www.charismamag.com/blogs/power-up/11480-lessons-from-a-chicken.

refuge." Ruth said, "When I think of those baby chicks running to their mother, I realize it is under His wings that we may seek refuge—*but we have to run to Him.*"[40]

Yes, in our lives when the hawks circle, God offers us comfort and safety. Boaz, in the book of Ruth, refers to the God of Israel to Ruth as the one "under whose wings you have come to take refuge" (2:12). Psalm 36:7 and 61:4 speak of taking refuge in the shadow or shelter of God's wings. One of my favorite insights into the heart of Jesus is when He cries out over Jerusalem, "O Jerusalem, Jerusalem. . . . How often would I have gathered your children together as a hen gathers her brood under her wings, and you were not willing!" (Matthew 23:37).

I wonder if there are times when God would like to have comforted me "under His wings," but instead of coming to Him, I depended on my own resources. It's something to think about, for when He covers us, the forces of hell cannot penetrate His protection.

Reflection ─────────────────────────

Who can you share this thought with today—perhaps by e-mail or a phone call? Take a few minutes to bless someone who needs help.

Conversation with God ─────────────

Lord, I'm running to You for both comfort and safety. Hide me under Your wings—close to Your heart.

───────────

40 Ibid.

Hope for Eternity

By Luisa Reyes-Ampil

Just as it is appointed for man to die once,
and after that comes judgment.

HEBREWS 9:27

South Koreans are creating a trend today that many would consider macabre. More than fifteen thousand visitors of all ages have "experienced death" at the Hyowon Healing Center by staging their own mock funerals. Dressed in traditional burial clothes, they lay inside their closed coffins for ten minutes. And what did this death experience do for the testers? According to them, it helped them evaluate their stressful lives, emphasizing emotional preparation for their own deaths. They were also taught how to say their good-byes and to get their wills in place.[41]

Can someone live with renewed hope after experiencing a mock funeral? Does it really matter if you are or are not prepared emotionally for your death? Would it be more helpful to think of the afterlife knowing that eternity really exists?

When a certain rich man died, he found himself " 'in Hades, being in torment' " (Luke 16:23). And far off, he saw Abraham with Lazarus, the poor man who used to lie at his gate covered with sores, before he, too, died. The rich man begged Abraham, "Have mercy on me, and send Lazarus to dip the end of his finger in water and cool my tongue, for I am in anguish in this flame" (v. 24).

---

41 "Well-Dying," *World Teen* (March–April 2016), 18.

Yes, Lazarus and the rich man were dead and not just in a mock death experience. But the rich man had had a choice and now faced the consequences in his death of how he had lived. It is very clear what eternal death and state of suffering lie before some of us. There is no way it can be avoided, no relief no matter how much you beg. But death is not just about lying in a coffin for ten minutes. After death our spirits will go on to feel the excruciating pain of eternal death if we end up on the wrong side of heaven.

But if you are interested in renewing the hope that your eternity will be spent in Jesus' presence, then come to Jesus and drink of the water that He gives, for it " 'will become in him a spring of water welling up to eternal life' " (John 4:14).

Reflection

What are your feelings about eternity?

Conversation with God

Help me, Lord, to remember that life may be short, but as a believer, I can look forward to an eternity with You.

Casting. . .

By Darlene Sala

*Casting all your anxieties on him,
because he cares for you.*

1 PETER 5:7

Here's a thought that challenges me: "Prayer is bringing your wishes and worries to God; faith is leaving them there." The prayer part is easy, but the faith part—that is, leaving our worries with God—is another matter, right?

Prayer—the way we bring our concerns to God—is almost an automatic reaction when we're in trouble. Even people who say they don't believe in God cry out frantically to Him when they are in a desperate situation. But it takes sincere faith to *leave* those anxieties with Him and trust that He is going to bring good out of even the most horrible of circumstances.

Sometimes when I'm really anxious about a situation, I'm hesitant to just leave it with God because that seems rather irresponsible. Shouldn't I be doing *something* to help solve the problem? Yet, the truth is, only God knows the future, so He is the only one who can provide the right solution. Continuing to worry means I don't really believe God is going to solve the problem.

Also, did you notice that Peter gives us the reason we should cast our anxieties on the Lord? He says we should do it *because He cares for us*. He feels concern for us the way a parent does for a hurting child.

The word *casting* in this verse is the same word used in Luke 19:35, where the crowds were casting their outer clothing on the colt that Jesus rode when He entered Jerusalem on the day we call Palm Sunday.[42] The idea is different from casting a fishing line into the water only to reel it in a few moments later. The meaning involves complete commitment of what is being cast, not bringing the problem to God in prayer only to take it back again on my own shoulders at the end of the prayer.

Reflection

Because You care so much for me, I can leave my concerns with You and know that You will take care of them better than I can.

Conversation with God

Lord, today I'm going to cast my anxieties on You and, by Your grace, leave them there.

---

42 W. E. Vine, *Vine's Expository Dictionary of New Testament Words* (McLean, VA: Mac Donald Publishing Company, n.d.), 174.

Check-in, Please!

By Luisa Reyes-Ampil

> *"In my Father's house are many rooms. If it were not so,*
> *would I have told you that I go to prepare a place for you?"*
> JOHN 14:2

For more than a decade I worked for two five-star hotels in the Philippines at the beginning of my career, spending the first five years at the front desk of one of these luxury establishments. Part of our work responsibilities included selecting rooms for arriving guests and making sure they were ready with amenities during check-in. All of the VIP guests were met by the hotel team, from the airport to the hotel, whereupon they were whisked straight to their suites for private registration.

Our heavenly Father owns the biggest and fanciest hotel we can imagine—with a star rating beyond the ability of The Leading Hotels and Preferred Hotels, organizations that represent some of the most distinguished luxury hotels around the world, to award. This hotel has the finest of all general managers: *Jesus Christ.* Jesus said, "And if I go and prepare a place for you, I will come again and will take you to myself, that where I am you may be also" (John 14:3). Jesus has already made sure that our individual rooms are prepared and ready for our arrival.

My stepdad, Pops, suffered severe brain trauma from an accidental fall. I and my siblings rushed to gather at the hospital's

ICU, to sing his favorite pop songs, hymns, and worship songs to him and bring to mind the special and funny memories we shared.

The time came when Fernando, my brother-in-law and pastor, personalized this Bible verse and said to Pops, "Don't worry about us now, Pops. We will be fine. *Go and claim the room Jesus has prepared for you!*" And right before our eyes, Pops's heart rate immediately dropped by half until it flatlined moments later as he joined Jesus in heaven.

How very true that our heavenly Father indeed has a reserved room for each one of us who profess faith in Jesus Christ! Jesus demonstrated this the night He arrived to pick up Pops—He came to bring Pops to His special hotel—heaven. How wonderful that we witnessed the moment when Pops finally said to Jesus, "*Check-in, please!*"

Reflection

Are you sure you have prepared yourself for an eventual check-in at our Father's home?

Conversation with God

Thank You for making Your Word come to life, confirming Your promise that You will come back for us!

When We Cannot See

By Bonnie Sala

*And we know that in all things God works for the good of those
who love him, who have been called according to his purpose.*
ROMANS 8:28 NIV

Childbirth is surely one of the most difficult times in any woman's
life. It's a time when a husband would want to provide the most
comfortable environment for his laboring wife. But the four
Gospels indicate that few comforts were available to Mary and
Joseph as they stopped in Bethlehem at a very vulnerable and
physically tough time.

Joseph could do little more than find clean straw for Mary
to rest upon and scoop the remnants of feed out of an animal
trough for her newborn. And Mary, without her mother or midwife
familiar to her, endured the agony of labor with the scent of
manure hanging in the air. We could easily imagine them filled
with fear and anxiety. "There was nowhere to lean," observed
missionary and author Elisabeth Elliot, "except the Everlasting
Arms. They had God's word, specially delivered by the angel
Gabriel."

But was *this* the way the Messiah, the Savior of all humankind
was to come? Had they misunderstood? Where was the angel
now? Where was God? "Weak things, lowly things, painful things,
silent things—the instinct of their faith told them God was in all
of them. . .God had given them His Word. Therefore, they moved

trustfully, quietly through each moment, God being in charge, God being in that moment,"[43] wrote Elliot.

Would we have trusted at a moment like that?

The shockingly humble beginning of Jesus' life here on earth wasn't what we would expect for the birth of the King of kings. Yet here we find great hope! Elliot explained:

> So it may be for us when God's order is the reverse of what we would expect. He is in each moment, in us, with us, as He is with the Holy Couple on their wearisome journey over the dusty roads and in the raw cattle shed. Should we expect to see how things are working together for our good? No, not yet. We see not yet. We only know.[44]

We are reminded that, when we cannot see, we go back to what we know: "in all things God works" (Romans 8:28 NIV).

Reflection

Has there been a time in your life when you thought you had heard God's voice loud and clear but you found yourself in a lonely, dark place, in unthinkable circumstances, in great confusion? Are you, or is someone you love, there now?

Conversation with God

Help me to remember what I know, while You work in all things!

43 Elisabeth Elliot, *Secure in the Everlasting Arms* (Ann Arbor, MI: Vine, 2002), 176.
44 Ibid.

Crossing Bridges
By Darlene Sala

"Therefore I tell you, do not worry about your life."
MATTHEW 6:25 NIV

My friend Sonya Goodson posted this on her Facebook page: "I have crossed many bridges that I never came to. . . ."

Oh, Sonya, so have I! And what a waste of time and emotional energy it has been!

I love to plan ahead. For instance, I think half the fun of taking a vacation trip is planning and anticipating all that I hope to enjoy. John Green wrote, "The pleasure isn't in doing the thing, the pleasure is in planning it."[45]

But in life, planning ahead can take a bad turn and very quickly become worry. When we see a problem looming on the horizon, we anticipate trouble. We want to try to "cross the bridge" ahead of time and see how things turn out. And have you noticed that we usually expect the worst-case scenario to happen?

It seems to me that mothers are especially good at this. Because it usually falls on us to plan the family activities, we quickly imagine the concussion Steven might suffer if he plays soccer. Or what terrible thing could happen if Susan goes with the church youth group on that mission trip to Africa. There we go again crossing bridges that we may never come to.

45 John Green, *Paper Towns* (New York: Dutton, 2008), 233.

Once when the disciples and Jesus crossed the Sea of Galilee in a storm, Jesus said to them, "Why are you so afraid? Do you still have no faith?" And when we have crossed a stormy Sea of Galilee in our lives, we often look back and say, "How silly of me, worrying as I did, when I could have saved so much trouble by turning the situation over to the Lord."

Let's ask God to help us walk step by step each day with Him and not to anticipate trouble. If and when you do come to a bridge you must cross, know that He will hold your hand, for He said, "When you pass through the waters, I will be with you; and when you pass through the rivers, they will not sweep over you" (Isaiah 43:2 NIV).

Reflection

" 'So do not fear, for I am with you; do not be dismayed, for I am your God. I will strengthen you and help you; I will uphold you with my righteous right hand' " (Isaiah 41:10 NIV).

Conversation with God

Because I can't see into the future, Lord, my first reaction is to worry. My prayer to You today is that old song,

> *There are things about tomorrow*
> *I don't seem to understand*
> *But I know who holds tomorrow*
> *And I know who holds my hand.*[46]

---

46 "I Know Who Holds Tomorrow," lyrics by Ira F. Stanphill, Wikipedia, accessed December 18, 2016, https://en.wikipedia.org/wiki/Ira_Stanphill.

One Day

By Luisa Reyes-Ampil

---

*So we are always of good courage. We know that while
we are at home in the body we are away from the Lord.*
2 CORINTHIANS 5:6

My friend Cookie posted this on her Facebook page accompanied
by a crying emoji: "My beloved sister, Becbec. I don't want to
bother you from the purest of bliss you are in right now. . .but I
wish we could be together just one more time."

Cookie and family had lost Becbec to cancer the year before.
She was fifty-six. Her journey took three years, but they didn't
forget to make wonderful memories along the way. Three months
before Becbec's home-going, they went to Hawaii for a four-day
reunion. Despite the pain, Becbec took part in the joys and
laughter. A month later they all traveled to New Jersey to see
Becbec one last time while reliving the recent Hawaii trip even
through the morphine haze. The last celebration she attended
was their mom's ninetieth birthday via Skype.

*For we know that if the tent that is our earthly home
is destroyed, we have a building from God, a house
not made with hands, eternal in the heavens. For in
this tent we groan, longing to put on our heavenly
dwelling, if indeed by putting it on we may not be found
naked. For while we are still in this tent, we groan, being*

burdened—not that we would be unclothed, but that we would be further clothed, so that what is mortal may be swallowed up by life. He who has prepared us for this very thing is God, who has given us the Spirit as a guarantee. (2 Corinthians 5:1–5)

There's the fine line between fighting and giving up that we will all have to walk. We fight for our family's cause just like Becbec did—who fought to see her youngest son graduate from medical school, to hold her second grandchild, and to enjoy their mom's birthday one more time. But eventually we will all have to give up the fight, to finally claim our rightful place with our Lord.

Losing a loved one—a spouse, a parent, a child, or a friend—is never easy, but God will continue to provide us comfort as we grieve our loss. One day, Cookie, the reunion will come!

Reflection

Are you walking through the valley right now because you lost a loved one? Take comfort in the get-together that is ahead.

Conversation with God

Thank You, Lord, that You will be with us through our grief and suffering.

I'm Afraid!

By Darlene Sala

"It is the LORD who goes before you. He will be with you;
he will not leave you or forsake you. Do not fear or be dismayed."
DEUTERONOMY 31:8

Courtney Ellis tells of the time her family was driving down the highway when a deer darted out from the bushes, colliding with their car before her dad even saw the animal. The airbags deployed. The car was totaled. But fortunately, no one was seriously hurt.

As the stunned family sat in the car gathering their wits about them, her dad suddenly shouted, "She's going to blow! Get out of the car!" The family hastily fled the vehicle. Terrified, Courtney's little sister took off running—down the centerline of the highway! What had been a serious situation instantly became critical.

Courtney's dad took off in pursuit, finally grabbed the little girl in his arms, and ran with her to the edge of the highway. Her little legs were still trying to run as he held her. Fright had become flight.

Isn't that the reaction of many of us when we're afraid? We panic. Sensing that there is nothing we can do to rescue ourselves, we try to run from the problem—instead of running *to* our heavenly Father. He is the one who can save us—often the only one who can get us out of the mess we're in.

What fearful situation are you facing right now? Is your home in chaos? Do you have a child or grandchild who is running from God? Is it the "C" word—dreaded cancer? Run *to* your heavenly Father, not *from* Him.

Don't wait another minute. Throw yourself into His arms and let Him comfort you as only He can. As the writer of Lamentations says, "This I call to mind, and therefore I have hope: The steadfast love of the LORD never ceases; his mercies never come to an end; they are new every morning; great is your faithfulness. 'The LORD is my portion,' says my soul, 'therefore I will hope in him'" (Lamentations 3:21–24).

Reflection

"Even though I walk through the valley of the shadow of death, I will fear no evil, for you are with me" (Psalm 23:4).

Conversation with God

I'm running to You, Lord, right now. Take me in Your arms and hear my heart cry.

Pools in the Valley
By Bonnie Sala

As they go through the Valley of Baca they make it a place of springs; the early rain also covers it with pools.
PSALM 84:6

Our journeys into grace take us to mountaintops and, yes, through the bottoms of deep, dry valleys. In Bible times pilgrims would journey by foot or mule over dusty roads and paths to Jerusalem, the city set on a hill, to worship at the temple. If you've ever had the chance to visit this part of the world, or been in a desert, you know how critical water is. The travelers in Psalm 84 couldn't carry enough water for the entire journey; you can be sure that they were looking urgently for a spring or stream for refreshment as they passed through the Valley of Baca (or the Valley of *Weeping*, as some translations read) on their way to Jerusalem.

There are times in our lives that feel spiritually dry. Prayers seem to bounce back; scripture fails to move us. We may feel like we are just going through the motions. It's discouraging. God knows this. In Isaiah, He said, "When the poor and needy search for water and there is none, and their tongues are parched from thirst, then I, the LORD, will answer them. I, the God of Israel, will never abandon them. . . . I will give them fountains of water in the valleys. I will fill the desert with pools of water. Rivers fed by springs will flow across the parched ground" (Isaiah 41:17–18 NLT).

Be encouraged, traveler! Here, God says *I will* four times! He will answer, He will never abandon, He will give refreshment. He is working in the dry valley. "I never would have been able to comfort anguished seekers if I myself had not been kept waiting for mercy," wrote the Victorian preacher Charles Spurgeon. "I have always felt grateful for distress because of the results afterward. Many saints whose experiences are published could never have written those books if they had not waited hungry and thirsty and full of soul sorrow. The spade of agony digs deep trenches to hold the water of life."[47]

Take heart in what God says *He will* do. Notice verse 6 of Psalm 84 that says, *"As they go through. . ."* Just keep walking. The believer's journey always finds its end in His grace.

Reflection _____

Have you gone through dry valleys? Are you in one now?

Conversation with God _____

Lord, I'm thirsty. Please exchange my soul sorrow for Your refreshment and mercy.

---

47 C. H. Spurgeon, quoted in "Beside Still Waters: Waiting for Mercy," *The Root and Bud*, June 8, 2011, accessed December 3, 2016, http://therootandbud.blogspot .com/2011/06/waiting-for-mercy.html.

Under a Heavy Load

*When you've
gone and done it,
He says come and rest!*

Have Trouble Saying No?
By Darlene Sala

If any of you lacks wisdom, let him ask God,
who gives generously to all without reproach.

JAMES 1:5

Do you have trouble saying no when you're asked to do something? If so, you probably find yourself too busy for your own good—or anyone else's. Mary Byers gives us an idea that will help. The technique is called "Five Times Why," and it's attributed to Taiichi Ohno, father of the Toyota Production System. Here's how it works. When someone asks you to do something and you're feeling overwhelmed, first ask yourself:

> **Why** am I feeling overwhelmed?
>> *Because I'm doing too much.*
> **Why** am I doing too much?
>> *Because I say yes to everything.*
> **Why** do I say yes to everything?
>> *Because I'm afraid to say no.*
> **Why** am I afraid to say no?
>> *Because I'm afraid they won't like me.*
> **Why** am I afraid they won't like me?
>> *Because I've never said no to them before, and I*
>> *don't know how they'll respond.*[48]

48 Mary M. Byers, *How to Say No and Live to Tell about It* (Eugene, OR: Harvest House, 2006), 63–64.

While your first response to why you're feeling overwhelmed is probably that you're doing too much, the Five Times Why exercise reveals the real reason that you say yes—because you're afraid people won't like you if you turn them down. Byers points out that Five Times Why encourages you to "go deeper than a surface understanding of a situation. . .which often leads to new insight and understanding."[49]

God has promised to give us wisdom when we need it. James tells us, "If any of you lacks wisdom, let him ask God, who gives generously to all without reproach" (James 1:5). When we have a decision to make, however, we need to be willing to give up our own desires and ask God to make His will plain. Then when we feel certain of God's will, we must be willing to do it—even if that means saying no to a friend's request.

Reflection

Doing God's will does not necessarily mean doing more.

Conversation with God

Lord, You know I have a hard time saying no when people ask me to help. I'm afraid they'll think I'm selfish or uncaring and they'll reject me. But You know that right now I have more to do than I can handle. Help me to say no in the kindest possible way and not worry about whether people like me or not.

---

49 Ibid., 66.

Redemption

By Bonnie Sala

> *"Everything is meaningless," says the*
> *Teacher, "completely meaningless!"*
> ECCLESIASTES 1:2 NLT

Only forty-three when he suddenly died in Egypt from appendicitis, Oswald Chambers was a no-nonsense British chaplain in World War I. A month before his death in 1917, he gave a series of talks to the troops stationed at the YMCA hut at Zeitoun. His text was a bit different—the book of Ecclesiastes. "Everything is meaningless," it begins.

The theme hardly seems inspiring for men facing the gruesome horrors of war, the likes of which had never been seen. And yet, there was a stark realism to his sermons that matched the nightmare the world was living through. "The basis of things," Chambers wrote, "is not rational, but tragic," and this is the view of life that the Bible actually presents us with. "There ought to be no sin, no war, no devil, no sickness, no injustice; but these things are!"[50]

This is real life. This is the life that each of us, in some painful way, knows. My friend Dana knows it. Her handsome son, a professional athlete, fought for two years before dying of cancer at the age of twenty-eight. My friend Laura knows it,

---

50 Oswald Chambers, *Shade of His Hand* (Fort Washington: Christian Literature Crusade, 1936), 4.

for she has grieved through miscarriage after miscarriage, her arms empty. "In true thinking of things as they actually are there is always a bedrock of unmitigated sadness,"[51] said Chambers.

But this is where the Bible differs from any other religious text. "The Bible reveals that the basis of things is tragic and the way out is by Redemption." The Bible, and the faith of the Christian, addresses life *as it is* and says there is only one God and "His name is Jesus Christ and in Him we see mirrored what the human race will be like on the basis of Redemption."[52] "For now we see through a glass, darkly; but then face to face" (1 Corinthians 13:12 KJV).

We can't pretend that man hasn't made a mess. But God acknowledged the reality that His creation chose and made a way for us and all of creation to be redeemed! Apart from relationship with God, yes, "everything is meaningless." But, "Jesus Christ is the One Who can transmute everything we come across."[53] He changes everything.

Reflection

Is there loss or pain in your life that you are waiting on Jesus to redeem?

Conversation with God

Father, thank You that You are with us in this world as it is, but thank You that You will make all things new for the believer in Your time and for all eternity!

---

51 Ibid., 5.
52 Ibid.
53 Ibid.,10.

At the End of Your Rope

By Darlene Sala

And whatever you do, in word or deed,
do everything in the name of the Lord Jesus.
COLOSSIANS 3:17

"Just do the next thing" was the advice missionary author Elisabeth Elliot gave to her daughter, Valerie, when she called on the phone one morning at a point of desperation. A homeschooling mother of eight, Valerie had reached the end of her resources. "What do I do, Mom? I just can't go on."

"Just do the next thing!" her mother counseled her.

I can totally relate to Valerie. And I don't even have eight kids! But many a time I've been at that breaking point when I felt I couldn't clean up another sticky mess or tackle another pile of laundry or answer another question from a four-year-old. But "do the next thing"? Most times I felt more like sitting down to watch a mindless movie on TV than doing the next thing.

Now, let me be honest, I do like to make lists. Somehow having a list of what needs to be done and crossing off what actually gets done gives me a great sense of satisfaction. But how do we decide what should be the "next thing"?

Okay, what is it you absolutely *have* to accomplish today? I mean, if you don't get another thing done today, what's the one thing that *must* be done? Then, leave everything else and get started on that one thing that is essential. True, you may never finish another item on your list, but you will have done the one thing that was crucial.

Colossians 3:23–24 gives purpose to what we do: "Whatever you do, work heartily, as for the Lord and not for men, knowing that from the Lord you will receive the inheritance as your reward. You are serving the Lord Christ."

I know, I know, some jobs seem so purposeless. You may clean up the sticky mess today only to have another mess to clean up tomorrow. But the fact that you did it for the Lord means He will reward you. Follow this advice, and at the end of the day you may still be tired, but you will have accomplished the most important task, and you'll know you've done your best.

Reflection

"The next thing" that needs to be done may not be easy, but tackling it first will mean I can soon cross it off my list.

Conversation with God

Please help me, Lord, to do the most important task first. You know how hard that is for me.

Getting to "Later On"
By Bonnie Sala

*No discipline seems pleasant at the time, but painful. Later on,
however, it produces a harvest of righteousness and peace for
those who have been trained by it. Therefore, strengthen your
feeble arms and weak knees. "Make level paths for your feet,"
so that the lame may not be disabled, but rather healed.*
HEBREWS 12:11–13 NIV

"A harvest of righteousness and peace" is what Hebrews 12:11–13
says that discipline produces in the life of the believer. Of
course, it prefaces these words with the phrase *later on*. Have
you ever thought, *Lord, please help me to make it to "later on"*?
I certainly have.

"Therefore," the passage continues, "strengthen your feeble
arms and weak knees." I don't think we are talking about a
workout at the gym here, so how is this done—this strengthening
that trains us to get through the unpleasant discipline of the
moment, of today, to the harvest of righteousness and peace
coming later on? I asked myself this as I journaled several years
ago, and here's the answer I wrote: "I really can't muster up any
strength on my own—it isn't there. Period." So, I kept reading.

Verse 13 of the chapter says, "Make level paths for your
feet." "How can I do that?" I mused. What constitutes a "level
path"? If I am traveling this path from the discipline of today
to the harvest of later on, I do want that path to be as level as

possible! I thought about my tendency to go overboard in busily meeting the needs and wants of my husband and children so that I would receive love and appreciation, neglecting my legitimate personal needs for time alone, to create beauty, to exercise, to think long and hard about what God wanted to whisper to me in that season. And the result: I would eventually become mean. Just overwhelmed and *mean*!

The most level path for me is a life that *is not too busy*. When I am too busy, I don't take care of myself, I get stressed and grumpy, and sin abounds. When I am too busy, it means I'm missing out on time spent relaxing in the presence of Jesus, being reoriented by Him. Yes, it's the only way I'll ever get to the "later on" of Hebrews!

Reflection

What would making a level path for your feet look like in your life?

Conversation with God

Teach me to order my steps, Lord, so that I am walking a level path and can learn from whatever discipline You lovingly choose to shape me with today. Thank You in advance for the coming harvest!

Hopeless?
By Darlene Sala

May the God of hope fill you with all joy and peace in believing,
so that by the power of the Holy Spirit you may abound in hope.
ROMANS 15:13

If you feel that the situation you face is hopeless, you may fall into a pit of depression that can even lead to thoughts of suicide. After all, you reason, if there is no hope of change, why continue living?

That is why at Guidelines International Ministries we receive letters like this one from a lady who wrote, "On Saturday I was so depressed that I wanted to kill myself. This is not the first time, either." Another, who struggles with an alcoholic father and a husband who abuses drugs and alcohol, wrote, "I have lost my hope." A third said, "I have been going to church for over eight years, and I've backslidden to a point where I didn't think I could ever receive grace in God's eyes again. My sins were so great. . .that I often felt suicide was the only way."

In the book of Romans the apostle Paul calls God "the God of hope." He wrote, "May the God of hope fill you with all joy and peace as you trust in him, so that you may overflow with hope by the power of the Holy Spirit" (Romans 15:13 NIV).

Do you know the God of hope, the one Paul was talking about? Or is the God you know an angry God who determines to beat the daylights out of all of us who mess up our lives, unable to control the circumstances we face? I want to assure you that where there is God, there is hope. Today if you are at the end of your rope, throw yourself on Him. No situation you face is beyond His help.

Reflection

Charles Allen, a great Scottish preacher, pointed out that the real profanity of man is not some swear words we use. The most profane word we use. . .is the word *hopeless*. When you say a situation or a person is hopeless, you are slamming the door in the face of God.[54]

Conversation with God

Today, Lord, I throw myself on You. I give up trying to solve my own problems. I will trust fully in You. I acknowledge You are my only hope.

---

54 Charles L. Allen, *All Things Are Possible through Prayer* (Grand Rapids, MI: Revell, 1958, 2003), 51.

Paula's Story

By Darlene Sala

Do not hide your face from me in the day of my distress!
Incline your ear to me; answer me speedily in the day when I call!
PSALM 102:2

In desperation, she grabbed two bottles—a bottle of whiskey and a bottle of pills—and headed to the beach. At last she would end her pain. Two years of struggle and depression since her divorce had destroyed every thread of hope for the future. Why keep trying?

As she sat there on the sand ready to end it all, in a desperate attempt to find an alternative she called out to God for a sign that He was there. A few moments later a magnificent ray of sunshine broke through the clouds and fell exactly on the spot where she was, enveloping her in its warmth and light. Through the fog of her pain, she knew beyond the shadow of a doubt that God was reaching out to her. Standing to her feet, she began to walk, and as she did, miraculously the ray of sun followed her. She was stunned. "God, I give up. You can have my life. I turn it over to You." Paula told me, "I shall never stop thanking Him for saving my life that day!"

Does God always reach out to people in such a dramatic way? No, not always. But He does reach out to every single one of us through the truth of His Word that says, " 'Call upon me in the day of trouble; I will deliver you' " (Psalm 50:15), and " 'Whoever comes to me I will never cast out' " (John 6:37).

Perhaps today you are at such a point of desperation. You don't want to go on living unless something changes. You, like Paula, may even have considered taking your life rather than enduring the circumstances that you face.

Right now call out to God. He may give you a visible sign of His presence. Or instead you may simply sense His tender love reaching out to enfold you in a dimension you have never sensed before. Come to the One who can change your life forever and give you hope.

Reflection

"He regards the prayer of the destitute and does not despise their prayer" (Psalm 102:17).

Conversation with God

Dear God, I am at the end of my rope. I don't think I can go on another day unless You help me. I confess my desperate need for You and ask You to take over my life. Come into my heart and change me. I ask You in Jesus' name, amen.

Feel Like Giving Up on God?
By Darlene Sala

What god is great like our God?
PSALM 77:13

Asaph was discouraged—so discouraged, in fact, that he had about given up on God. He asks five questions that convey the despair he is feeling: "Will the Lord spurn forever, and never again be favorable? Has his steadfast love forever ceased? Are his promises at an end for all time? Has God forgotten to be gracious? Has he in anger shut up his compassion?" (Psalm 77:7–9). Asaph tells us he cried aloud and couldn't sleep. He was in a bad way!

One of the reasons I love the Bible is that it is so honest. If a person was fed up with God, you'll read about it in God's Word. I think it's an indication that God wants us to be honest with Him about our feelings. If we're ever going to have an intimate relationship with God, it has to be based on honesty between us and Him.

Maybe you're feeling the same way today as Asaph did. You're wondering if God has forgotten you, because you have a big need in your life that is still unmet. You've almost given up on God because He hasn't answered your prayer yet. If so, don't stop with the first part of Psalm 77, because Asaph goes on to give us the solution. Yes, he found an answer to his deep discouragement.

He writes, " 'I will appeal to this, to the years of the right hand of the Most High.' I will remember the deeds of the LORD; yes, I will remember your wonders of old. I will ponder all your work, and meditate on your mighty deeds. . . . What god is great like our God?" (vv. 10–13). And then he goes on to list some of the wonders God had done in the past.

Say, what wonders has God done in *your* past that you haven't thought about lately? Did He bring you through a complex situation at work? Heal your baby? Supply a financial need that you thought was impossible to meet? He is still the same God today.

Hold on! Know that He hasn't stopped loving you or forgotten you. In His time He will answer with exactly what you need, for there's no other god like Him!

Reflection

What a short memory I have for what God has done for me in the past! So quickly I forget that He never changes.

Conversation with God

Lord, I'm pouring out my true feelings to You. Help me to hold on a little longer until You meet my need.

Done

By Bonnie Sala

He heals the brokenhearted and binds up their wounds.
PSALM 147:3

There sometimes comes a time when a person is just done. *Done in.* Kay Bruner was done. The "thirty-something missionary lady" stood in the middle of a gravel road, on a hill, in the highlands of Papua New Guinea and said, "I can't do this anymore." [55] So they gave her a little blue pill and put her to bed. When she woke up, she wanted to die.

Elijah did, too. He and God had pulled out all the stops against the crazy-wicked King Ahab and Queen Jezebel. Elijah had called down fire from heaven and personally put to death 850 prophets of Baal and Asherah (1 Kings 18). But Jezebel was unfazed by the show and vowed to have Elijah's head by the next day. Terrified, Elijah ran and ran, sat down under a tree, told God, "Take my life!" and went to sleep.

But when God's beloved are *done*, God does two things: He comes in wisdom and He comes in just the right way. Elijah's needs were first physical. So God sent an angel who cooked for Elijah, touched him, and put him back to sleep (1 Kings 19:5–6). God doesn't even begin to deal with Elijah's thinking until he'd rested and gotten to a cave on the Mountain of God...and then slept again.

---

55 Kay E. Bruner, *As Soon as I Fell: A Memoir* (Kindle, 2014), prologue.

The next morning there was the earthquake, the wind, and the fire. But that wasn't what Elijah needed; he needed the "still small voice" (1 Kings 19:12 KJV). He came to Moses in the fire, and He came in the wind to the apostles at Pentecost, but Elijah needed a whisper.

Kay Bruner needed to be listened to. All of her life, first as a missionary kid and then serving as a missionary along with her husband, she'd put her feelings on hold, pleasing, serving, suffering, trying so, so hard. Deeply isolated on remote islands of the South Pacific, she'd struggled to do language studies; Bible translation; and birth, raise, and homeschool four kids, with few supportive relationships. God had said, yes, she was *done* with living like that, so He sent an "earthquake," in the revelation of her husband's pornography addiction. God used the crisis to bring healing to both Kay and her husband—today she is a licensed professional counselor.

Reflection _____

Are you anywhere near *done* today?

Conversation with God _____

You know just what I need today, Father. Thank You for Your perfect, intimate love.

God in My Busy-ness
By Darlene Sala

But grow in the grace and knowledge
of our Lord and Savior Jesus Christ.
2 PETER 3:18

"If I have 1,001 things to do every day, how can I grow in my relationship with the Lord when sometimes a quick prayer is all I have time for?" my friend asked me.

A relevant question! Especially with the busy lives all of us experience these days. Is the answer to get up earlier so we have quiet time with the Lord? Maybe. Or how about learning to say no to some of the many requests for our time? Perhaps. But more important, I think, is bringing God into the details of our days.

That idea is not original with me, I assure you. There is a man who lived in the 1600s who is famous for doing just that. He is known as Brother Lawrence, the name he took when he joined a Carmelite monastery in Paris. Assigned to kitchen duty, he developed an intimate relationship with God by bringing God into his daily duties. Here's what he wrote:

> *The time of business does not differ with me from*
> *the time of prayer; and in the noise and clatter of my*
> *kitchen, while several persons are at the same time*
> *calling for different things, I possess God in as great*
> *tranquility as if I were on my knees.*[56]

56 Brother Lawrence, "Brother Lawrence Quotes," AZ Quotes, accessed August 10, 2016, http://www.azquotes.com/author/18695-Brother_Lawrence.

He furthermore described how to put this into practice:

[God] does not ask much of us, merely a thought of Him from time to time, a little act of adoration, sometimes to ask for His grace, sometimes to offer Him your sufferings, at other times to thank Him for the graces, past and present, He has bestowed on you, in the midst of your troubles to take solace in Him as often as you can.[57]

No, we can't always sit around with a Bible in our lap or be on our knees for hours at a time. But we can communicate with God moment by moment as we work. As my daughter Bonnie says, "Make sure you keep spiritually 'nibbling' daily when a 'sit-down dinner' isn't possible!"

P.S. I highly recommend that you get a copy of Brother Lawrence's book, *The Practice of the Presence of God*. It could change your life.

Reflection

"There is not in the world a kind of life more sweet and delightful, than that of a continual conversation with God; those only can comprehend it who practice and experience it." —Brother Lawrence[58]

Conversation with God

Lord, let today be the beginning of a deeper, more intimate relationship with You.

---

57 Brother Lawrence, quoted in "The Practice of the Presence of God Quotes," Goodreads, accessed August 10, 2016, https://www.goodreads.com/work/quotes/2133549-the-practice-of-the-presence-of-god.
58 Brother Lawrence, quoted in "Brother Lawrence Quotes," Goodreads, accessed August 10, 2016, https://www.goodreads.com/author/quotes/66573.Brother_Lawrence.

Relationships in the Real

So...about that love your neighbor stuff!

The Dance

By Luisa Reyes-Ampil

"Do two walk together, unless they have agreed to meet?"
AMOS 3:3

Wedding receptions often feature an awkward groom trying to keep up with the music as he dances with his new bride, whose steps are perfectly matched to the music. We laugh but excuse this almost-fiasco. After all, dancing either comes naturally or not. And a couple of lessons will not make you a dancer!

Terri and Bill are premarital counselors with Marriage by God. They were our marriage mentors.

"I know you love to dance, Luisa," Terri said in one session. "Imagine you and Ken in *Dancing with the Stars*. Ken is leading you. He twirls you. He dips you. His strength showcases your grace."

Hmmm. . . I listened with much interest because I do love to dance and understand it very well. I looked at Ken, and he seemed a little lost in the picture.

"Now the music conductor is Jesus Christ. The band is the Holy Spirit playing perfectly and you need to be in sync to Him. The judge is God, watching your moves because He gets to score the two of you in the end," Terri continued. I was wrapped up in this and had a smile on my face. I nodded as I saw parallels.

"Let's say you trip. Ken is there to catch you. And you don't stop dancing because of a misstep. You continue until the end!"

Yes, marriage can be likened to a dance. There are points when the music is playing softly and graceful basic steps are all you need. Everything is so easy to follow. You just move your right foot first, then your left foot next. Married life can be in that sweet spot.

But the music picks up and it's time for the more complicated moves to be performed. We might struggle with the leaps and jumps. *Will my spouse be able to catch me? Should I trust him with my life?* The answer is yes! You can't quit now. The beautiful part of the dance and the accompanying music are just building up! Trust each other and hold on to each other tight.

Whew! Ken and I went through our "rehearsals" with Terri and Bill as our "dance" coaches and were excited to learn the steps. When the curtain rose on our special day, we were ready to perform as one before the Conductor, Band, and Judge!

Reflection

Are you in sync with your spouse, or do you have to make some adjustments in the steps?

Conversation with God

Teach me and my spouse to come to You often, Lord, so we can be in harmony.

Submit???

By Darlene Sala

Wives, submit to your own husbands, as to the Lord.
EPHESIANS 5:22

Women, do you hate that verse? Well, maybe *hate* is too strong a word. But do you wish God had not put that verse in the Bible?

A friend asked me, "How do I submit to my husband as to the Lord while ensuring that I do not lose my individuality nor end up with the personality of a doormat?" It's a fair question. No woman wants to end up feeling like a slave to her husband, or as my friend put it, "a doormat" for him to wipe his feet on.

Marriage was never meant to be an arrangement where the husband is the slave master and the wife is the servant. God used marriage as a picture of His relationship with us as believers—an intimate love relationship where He wants nothing to come between us and Him. It's just as if you're going to have a parade of, say, two cars; one of them has to go first. And that's where God puts husbands—in front, leading the way, taking the responsibility for provision and safety in the relationship. And wives are to follow their leadership in what God intended to be a relationship of love.

But God doesn't give instruction only to wives. Three verses later in the same chapter, you find a command for husbands: "Husbands, love your wives, just as Christ also loved the church and gave Himself for her" (Ephesians 5:25 NKJV). If a man truly loves his wife, he will want the best for her and be willing to sacrifice for her. He will want her to develop and use her talents and abilities. He will want her to feel loved and cared for. I could go on and on.

Don't miss the summary at the end of the chapter: "Let each one of you love his wife as himself, and let the wife see that she respects her husband" (Ephesians 5:33). Love and respect—the perfect balance in a marriage.

The problem comes when we "read each other's mail," so to speak. The wife says, "You're supposed to love me like Christ loved the church." And the husband says, "Shut up and submit!" Wrong! Let's each concentrate on unselfishly fulfilling our part of the agreement, keeping love supreme.

Reflection

"Let us not love with words or speech but with actions and in truth" (1 John 3:18 NIV).

Conversation with God

Lord, help my marriage to be a picture to others of Your love for all of us who are believers. Help us always to communicate lovingly while we work out our differences.

Best Friends Forever—or Maybe Not

By Bonnie Sala

The righteous choose their friends carefully.
PROVERBS 12:26 NIV

The teen movie *Mean Girls*, written by comedian Tina Fey, became a cult classic for its depiction of high school female cruelty, cliques, and quips. The movie succeeded for a variety of reasons, but it obviously struck a chord: we women know that we can be horrible to one another, and we've all experienced some degree of treachery in navigating female friendships.

Radio host Anita Lustrea, author of *What Women Tell Me*, described trying to find a "best friend" for much of her life. From wanting someone to play with, to struggling through the misfit feelings of junior high and high school, even through college and into her work life, it was "best friends forever—or maybe not." Finding a good friend, a safe friend, a sister in Christ, can be difficult. But important.

When women ask Lustrea how to find a friend who can be trusted, she gives recommendations from Christian psychologists Henry Cloud and John Townsend, who say that a safe person does three things:

1. Draws us closer to God
2. Draws us closer to others
3. Helps us become the real person God created us to be.[59]

59 Anita Lustrea, *What Women Tell Me: Finding Freedom from the Secrets We Keep* (Grand Rapids, MI: Zondervan, 2010), 33.

The Bible has much to say about friends and friendship. "Two are better than one" (Ecclesiastes 4:9). "There is a friend who sticks closer than a [sister]" (Proverbs 18:24), and "A friend loves at all times" (Proverbs 17:17). There are also stories of great friendships, such as Ruth and Naomi and Jonathan and David. We know that God made us for relationship, so His promise to meet all of our needs would include our need for friendship.

A good friend, then, is something we can ask our Father for. However, your next friend may not be the person you expected. One listener of Lustrea's radio program wrote in admitting that she was surprised by God's gift. She wrote: " 'Our cleaning lady at work is becoming a very dear friend. Who knew? Others may pass her by as she carries a mop and broom, but I'm finding a wonderful prayer partner in her!' "[60] Of course, that's just like God to provide for our needs in ways we would never have thought of!

Reflection

Have you struggled in friendships with other women? Do you need a friend badly today?

Conversation with God

I do ask You, Father, for women to come alongside me as I come alongside them in friendships that draw us closer to You, to each other, and that draw me closer to being the woman You created me to be.

60 Ibid., 59.

Our Selfish World

By Luisa Reyes-Ampil

Give her of the fruit of her hands,
and let her works praise her in the gates.

PROVERBS 31:31

"I love kids. I ache for kids. But I love my life more,"[61] said popular Hollywood comedian, actress, producer, and writer Sarah Silverman. She is known for addressing controversial topics such as sexism and racism delivered with sarcasm in her stand-up acts.

Sarah Silverman is just one of the many women right now who love life. Or perhaps I should restate that latter part: *who love themselves.* "Some 15.3% of U.S. women aged 40 to 44 were childless [by choice] in June 2014, up from 15.1% in 2012,"[62] reads a 2015 blog from the *Wall Street Journal.* As more and more women enter the workforce and find success in their professions, marriage and children take a back seat and are postponed until a more convenient time.

Women today seem to have a blurry vision of God's original perspective and design. We like to live stressful lives by cramming our days with more things to accomplish and less time to think about God's plan and purpose. Yes, we may be lauded for our

61 *"Dispatches/Quotables,"* World, February 6, 2016, 16.
62 Neil Shah, "More U.S. Women Are Going Childless," *Wall Street Journal*, April 7, 2015, accessed September 17, 2016, http://blogs.wsj.com/economics/2015/04/07/more-u-s-women-are-going-childless/.

achievements, but we still gripe about the lower paychecks. We complain about inequality because there are some things that we just can't seem to break into!

You know the gold standard: "She makes linen garments and sells them; she delivers sashes to the merchant. Strength and dignity are her clothing, and she laughs at the time to come. She opens her mouth with wisdom, and the teaching of kindness is on her tongue. She looks well to the ways of her household and does not eat the bread of idleness. Her children rise up and call her blessed; her husband also, and he praises her" (Proverbs 31:24–28).

I am not a woman basher nor am I saying that all women should be married. That is up to God! I just want to see us viewed for what we rightly are—beautiful, refined, hardworking, loving, peaceful, and everything else wonderful! I am sure that whatever our decisions about marriage and children, making those decisions from an unselfish heart will bring fulfillment that self-centeredness can never bring!

Reflection

Have you asked the Lord to choose the perfect role for you—whatever the combination of mother, wife, professional? He has promised to give wisdom.

Conversation with God

I ask, Lord, that You help me see myself as the woman You want me to be—full of Your purpose and doing Your will.

Letting Go
By Bonnie Sala

Let love be genuine. Abhor what is evil; hold fast to what is good.
ROMANS 12:9

Have you had to let go of someone you loved? An unfaithful spouse? A child who needed to experience the consequences of choices made?

"Going rogue" is the term the authors of *Letting Go* use to describe the rebellion of the wayward person. Originally used to describe elephants that had abandoned their roles in the herd for erratic and dangerous behavior, the wayward—those who have *gone rogue*—choose to ignore God's authority in their lives, choose a pattern of unrepentant sin, and walk away from roles of spouse, son or daughter, friend, employer or employee, and so on. "When a fool decides to reject God's voice, he'll stubbornly and inexplicably allow his life, job, marriage, family, children, money to go up in smoke."[63]

I've stood right there, in the smoke, not knowing how to even take the next breath. I've done all the things those who love the wayward do: enabled, been over-responsible, appeased. But God calls the lover of the wayward to a love that is strong enough to face evil.

---

63 Dave Harvey and Paul Gilbert, *Letting Go: Rugged Love for Wayward Souls* (Grand Rapids, MI: Zondervan, 2016), 47.

Loving like this is not simple or easy. To get here you need to experience that love yourself, a love so sturdy that it enables you to face your biggest fears—your dread of a loved one leaving you, your anxiety over the unknown, or your unspoken suspicion that this situation indicates you're one humongous failure.[64]

If God is calling you to let go of a wayward one you love, you can expect Him to provide the clarity, the direction, and the strength to do so. I needed the steadying assurance of God's Word at all times. "Guide my steps by your word," I prayed from Psalm 119:133 (NLT), "so I will not be overcome by evil." I needed His promise of strength (Psalm 18:32), of wisdom (James 1:5), of guidance from the Holy Spirit (John 16:13), and a sense of His presence (Acts 2:28). All these He freely gives!

You can trust Him with your wayward one and with your own broken heart.

Reflection

Is there a wayward one you love in your life?

Conversation with God

Lord, I give You those that I love, even those who have walked far from You. I trust You to lead me in letting them go into Your providence.

---

64 Ibid., 72.

Praying for Your Grown-Up Kids

By Darlene Sala

My dear children, for whom I am again in the
pains of childbirth until Christ is formed in you.
GALATIANS 4:19 NIV

Whoever said parenting ends when your son or daughter turns twenty-one never was a parent! You never quit caring. Once you are a parent, you are forever a parent.

My heart always feels a tug when I read Paul's heart cry in Galatians 4:19 (NIV): "My dear children, for whom I am again in the pains of childbirth until Christ is formed in you." Isn't that a good description of what you're feeling? Your concern for your kids' spiritual welfare feels exactly like childbirth. Yes, if you have a personal relationship with Jesus, you long for each of your kids to make progress on their journey into grace, too.

If you have an adult child who isn't living for God right now, your heart is breaking. No one ever has to remind you to pray for that son or daughter. He or she is number one on your prayer list. You cry out to God to see heart change that will affect every part of their life.

And so you pray for them—the most important ministry moms can have to their adult children. Lecturing them certainly isn't effective. Criticizing them only pushes them away. The beautiful thing about praying for your kids is that you are enlisting the Holy Spirit to work in their lives as only He can.

We try to help from the outside of their hearts. God works on the inside. How encouraging is that!

Paul recorded several prayers that I like to apply to my children—and grandchildren:

* "I keep asking that the God of our Lord Jesus Christ, the glorious Father, may give you the Spirit of wisdom and revelation, so that you may know him better" (Ephesians 1:17 NIV).

* "It is my prayer that your love may abound more and more, with knowledge and all discernment, so that you may approve what is excellent, and so be pure and blameless for the day of Christ, filled with the fruit of righteousness that comes through Jesus Christ, to the glory and praise of God" (Philippians 1:9–11).

How about taking one of these scriptures and begin praying it back to God for your kids today?

Reflection _____

Love means you want the very best for your kids. There's nothing you can want for them that is more valuable than a close personal relationship with the Lord. That's what God wants, too.

Conversation with God _____

Lord, my heart cry for my children and grandchildren is that they will follow You with all their heart.

One Thankful Mama

By Luisa Reyes-Ampil

One who sows righteousness gets a sure reward.
PROVERBS 11:18

I have been blessed to have twin daughters who did really well in school. They were both accelerated from third to fifth grade. They were two out of Ten Most Outstanding Students in middle school. In high school, Christelle was one of the California Scholarship Federation awardees. In college, Christiane graduated cum laude in business.

I can go on and on about my children, but they now have their own careers and I am not as privy to their accomplishments as I used to be. They don't need to see their mama publicly cheering for them anymore. *They've got this!*

God surprised me one day after I prayed for Him to "overwhelm me" with His presence as I wanted to see His power at work in my children's lives outside of our home. Christelle, a middle school science teacher, shared with me a student's letter to her.

> *Thank you for the 2 wonderful years of teaching you*
> *have done to me. You have not only taught me about*
> *astronomy or life science or physics or biology, you*
> *have taught me what it's like to enjoy your life and live*

it. You have shown me that when doing good for others, good will come back to you. . . . You have shown me it's okay to make a few errors in life but you can still learn from them for the next time. . . . Even when times are tough there are still jokes and laughs to be held in your class, which makes it my favorite. We can have fun and still get work done at the same time. . . . Your generous acts of kindness will pay off in the end and I hope you continue your career as a teacher to make the lives of other children as great as mine.

I know that as she faces her students in class, Christelle is applying some of the biblical concepts she has learned from the time she was nine and came to know the Lord. And God has shown her favor, judging from the gifts and letters and cards she brings home.

Thank You, Lord, for the assurance that You will bring the harvest in my children's lives!

Reflection

Every person needs to know what he or she is good at. Find something positive for each one in your family and build on it.

Conversation with God

Lord, how wonderful that You overwhelm us with Your presence, not just in our lives but in the lives of our children as well!

Better Together

By Bonnie Sala

*And let us consider how we may spur one
another on toward love and good deeds.*
HEBREWS 10:24 NIV

I'm learning two things on my journey about how God changes
me to be more and more like Him: He does it gradually over time,
and He uses others to help and encourage me along the way.

I've often envisioned the process of God removing layer
and layer of fleshly self from my character, much like a cook
peels off the outer dried layers before reaching the moist, usable
portions of an onion. But my friend Heather likens the process
to a good spring cleaning:

"At first, God used a 24-watt bulb and allowed me to 'clean
up' what I saw. Then He put in a 50-watt bulb and I was able to
attend to the clutter and dirt in the newly seen edges of my being.
[Now] I am ready and another lightbulb is inserted—and again,
I can work on the newly illuminated areas. As the light increases
in brightness, I see areas of disarray that I feel powerless to
attend to on my own."

Thankfully, we don't make this journey toward Christlikeness
alone, but with members of Christ's body—as Heather calls them,
her "support team":

*In the recesses of the room, I see that my support team
is not afraid or shocked by my mess. They lovingly pick*

up brooms, mops, and dustpans and begin to help me clean up the debris and broken pieces. God lovingly shines light in the areas that need attention and surrounds me with people that are helping me clean out the areas that are too difficult to tackle on my own. The more I lean into the light and the support of my team, the more I am able to step out of denial.[65]

"Spur one another on," the writer of Hebrews exhorts us. "Warn those who are lazy. Encourage those who are timid. Take tender care of those who are weak. Be patient with everyone," wrote Paul in 1 Thessalonians 5:14 (NLT). And Paul wanted the Colossian believers "to be encouraged and knit together by strong ties of love" (Colossians 2:2 NLT).

God works in each of us individually to change us. But He also uses His body, our *support team,* to encourage us! He gave us our sisters in Christ as companions for the journey.

Reflection

Are you in relationship with other sisters in Christ? If not, how can you connect?

Conversation with God

Thank You, Lord, that You never intended for me to journey alone. Help me to reach out when I need encouragement and to watch for my sisters who need encouragement so that we can journey well.

65 Personal conversation shared in a Bible study.

Words Get in the Way

By Luisa Reyes-Ampil

Death and life are in the power of the tongue,
and those who love it will eat its fruits.

PROVERBS 18:21

My then-fiancé, Ken, and I were texting one day.

> Ken: THEY'RE TAKING NAMES OF THOSE WILLING TO WORK SATURDAY.

> Me: IF YOU ARE OKAY WITH WORK, LET'S GO FOR IT!

> Ken: YES! LOANS AND MARRIAGE. . .HAHA

> Me: THAT SOUNDS SAD.

Ken's words inferred that we were spending much of our time working to earn money to pay for our wedding. Some wonderful things get lost in translation when we don't think about our delivery as carefully as we should, and our words turn to something negative. Actually, Ken, who owned his own home that he renovated before our wedding day, was referring to his mortgage, not a loan for the wedding. We definitely did not borrow money or go overboard with our wedding budget—a laughably small amount to many!

I know full well the power of words! I raised my kids as a single mom for most of their lives. When I arrived tired from work and homework was not entirely done, with dinner still to prepare, scathing words sometimes spilled from my mouth. My girls would flinch and scramble to get the job done—to cool me down. I have asked for forgiveness more times than I can count, but it was sometimes difficult to do damage control.

How many times have I hurt my girls and other people I love with my *un-choicest* words? What of those who just happened to be in my path when I was angry and they didn't know what just hit them? How about God, when I thought He didn't care enough to answer my prayers and I said things that He didn't deserve?

God taught us the power of life in words as well. "Blessed is the one. . .whose delight is in the law of the LORD, and who meditates on his law day and night" (Psalm 1:1–2 NIV). I am sure that if we fill our hearts and minds with God's Word, there will be less room for a slip of the tongue.

I love you very much, Christiane and Christelle! I know it's not too late for you to hear me say this again and again!

Reflection

Have you said "I love you" to your spouse and children recently? Why not surprise them with these three important words instead of your usual anger?

Conversation with God

Thank You, Lord, that You search our hearts and You understand our emotions that often mislead us. Take over our tongues so we can praise You in everything we say.

Loving the Life You Never Wanted

By Bonnie Sala

*I have learned in whatever situation I am to be content. I know
how to be brought low, and I know how to abound. In any
and every circumstance, I have learned the secret of
facing plenty and hunger, abundance and need.*

PHILIPPIANS 4:11–12

I sat across the desk from a lawyer on my birthday and signed
the papers. Divorced. I was getting divorced. In my family, this
didn't happen. But it was happening. To me. I was living the life
I never wanted.

There were many years in the life of Joseph when he was
living the life he never wanted. Once the favorite son, he found
himself first thrown in a pit by all of his brothers, sold into
slavery, successful in his job, falsely accused, thrown into prison,
praised, and then forgotten. Finally, he was promoted to the most
powerful position in Egypt, under only Pharaoh. And what does
the Bible say about *every* season of Joseph's life? *The Lord was
with Joseph.* Whether in prison or in power, Joseph had hope
because of the Lord's presence (Genesis 39).

Only God could have written a life story like Joseph's! And
yet, God is writing the "story" of the life of every believer. "If you
love and follow Jesus," says Marshall Segal, "God always writes a
better story for you than you would write for yourself. The 'better'
is based on this: God himself is the best, most satisfying thing
you could ever have or experience, and, therefore, fullness of life

is ultimately found not in any earthly success or relationship or accomplishment, but in your proximity to God through faith."[66]

I would never have experienced that closeness to God in *my version* of my life story. I would never have been desperate for Him, would never have said, "I used to wander off until you disciplined me; but now I closely follow your word" (Psalm 119:67 NLT).

Do I love the life I never wanted? In some ways, yes. John Piper says, "When we have little and have lost much, Christ comes and reveals himself as more valuable than what we have lost. And when we have much and are overflowing in abundance, Christ comes and he shows that he is far superior to everything we have."[67]

The secret is Him in me, and there is now far more of Him than there ever would have been if I was living the life I "always" wanted.

Reflection _____

Have you experienced the secret of loving the life you never wanted?

Conversation with God _____

God, thank You that You are the one writing my story. Help me to remember that my hope is in You, not me, nor in a different set of circumstances!

---

66 Marshall Segal, "Love the Life You Never Wanted," Desiring God, February 16, 2016, accessed November 23, 2016, http://www.desiringgod.org/articles/love-the-life-you-never-wanted.

67 John Piper, "What Is the Secret of Joy in Suffering?" Desiring God, April 6, 2015, accessed November 23, 2016, http://www.desiringgod.org/articles/what-is-the-secret-of-joy-in-suffering.

The Announcement

By Luisa Reyes-Ampil

"Be still, and know that I am God."
PSALM 46:10

"I am moving to Colombia, Mom," my daughter announced one early Monday morning as I was preparing my lunch for work. "When?" I immediately responded, in a state of shock. "In two weeks," she said.

Tears started streaming down my face and questions crowded my mind. *Why is my daughter giving up her life in the US? What will she do in a country whose language is not our first language? Who do we know there who I can count on to help her if anything goes wrong?*

The evening of the announcement, I could not sleep. I was full of fear and worry. I feared that Christiane was making an ungodly choice, so I worried that she would come to harm and not be able to get any help at all when that happened. I could not stop my tears as I begged the Lord to bring me peace and comfort. By 2:00 a.m., He brought the calm and assured me that He is still in charge. What I hope and cannot do for my daughter, God can do. I had been asking the Lord for His will in both of my daughters' lives in my daily prayers.

And so she left. I heard from her when she needed my help—mostly financial in nature. My mind wanted to fill in the gaps, but I had to set aside my fear and worry and hold on to God's truth because He told me so. Before she left, she had written me a letter, and I reread it every single day she was away. She wrote, "I will appreciate all the things you have done and given more so now that I will be on my own. . . . I love you."

Psalm 46:10 was a constant reminder to me to "be still, and know that I am God." He knows the beginning and the end of each of our life stories. He whispered to me that He will take care of my daughter because He is doing the same for me. *Don't stop praying, Luisa!* That was my comfort and peace!

Seven months later Christiane arrived back in the US. When I picked her up at the airport, I could feel in the tightness of her embrace and the tears streaming down her face how much she missed her family. She's back! Thank You, Lord!

Reflection

What startling announcement did you receive recently that you need to trust the Lord for?

Conversation with God

In times of fear and worry, help me remember to "be still, and know that [You are] God."

Whose Luggage Are You Carrying?
By Bonnie Sala

So then each of us will give an account of himself to God.
ROMANS 14:12

Sometimes while we journey along with those we love, we get confused. Boy, is there ever a lot to care about and often—although we know it's sin—to *worry about*. The details, needs, and problems in our lives and in the lives of those we love become overwhelming.

Talk about struggling under a heavy load. Aren't we women specialists in this? But God's Word says we will only give an account for *ourselves*. We may need to get some clarity as to what "luggage" belongs to whom:

* If a person has a problem, a feeling, or a self-defeating behavior, that is their property, not ours.

* If someone has acted and experienced a particular consequence, both the behavior and the consequence belong to that person.

* If someone is in denial or cannot think clearly on a particular issue, that confusion belongs to them. So does their relationship with God.

* People's hopes, dreams, and choices are their property. Their guilt, their happiness, and their misery belong to them, too. Not us.

What belongs to me?

* My behavior, problems, feelings, happiness, misery, hopes, dreams, and choices

* My ability to love, care, nurture

* How I allow others to treat me

* My relationship with God[68]

Now what if you've already packed a bunch of someone else's stuff in your luggage? "If something isn't ours," says Melody Beattie, "we don't take it. If we take it, we learn to give it back. Let other people have their property, and learn to own and take good care of what's ours."[69] Yes, "We are each responsible for our own conduct," Galatians 6:5 (NLT) reminds us.

"But, what if I can *see* that what my loved one is doing will end in *disaster*?" you cry. As shocking as it may seem, God doesn't actually need our help in dealing with problems in the lives of others! Prayer allows us to express our concern and love for another to our Father—who has the sole power to act in that person's life, according to His perfect timing and in His perfect way.

Reflection

Whose property have you been carrying that you need to give over to your Father?

Conversation with God

Father, help me to concentrate on my own conduct and relationship with You and leave those I love in Your hands.

---

68 Melody Beattie, *The Language of Letting Go: Hazeldon Meditation Series* (Center City, MN: Hazelden, 2009), May 13 reading, accessed December 27, 2016, http://amzn.to/2if4Eew.
69 Ibid.

The Pendant

By Luisa Reyes-Ampil

"The LORD watch between you and me,
when we are out of one another's sight."
GENESIS 31:49

My dad, Louie, is a very sentimental and thoughtful father. He likes to give his daughters precious gifts. The one unique gift he gave to each daughter that usually attracts people's attention is a half-coin gold pendant—the mizpah. Each daughter received an identical half coin that completes his half coin.

I never gave much thought to what was written on it when I first received it. It was just a pendant, like any other piece of jewelry I owned. And because I didn't know Jesus Christ then, I did not know that the words on the half coin came from the Bible. Here's the story.

In Bible times Laban and Jacob came to a crossroads in their relationship, causing Jacob and his household to flee. It was a few days later when his absence was discovered by Laban. Laban pursued him because Jacob's wives, Leah and Rachel, who were Laban's daughters, were part of this hasty departure.

Finally Laban and Jacob came to a peaceful agreement. At their parting, Laban said, "The LORD watch between you and me, when we are out of one another's sight" (Genesis 31:49). The time had come for Laban to be separated from his daughters, but God would be watching over everyone.

I like that thought! Our dad didn't give us the pendants when we married. He gave them to us when we moved to the US permanently, while he stayed behind in the Philippines. Surely it was bittersweet for our dad to be separated from us. He realized, however, that the time had come when he couldn't physically watch over us because of the great distance, but God could!

I still wear my pendant occasionally. It has more meaning for me today knowing that our dad's best intentions are always to take care of us no matter how old we are or how far away we are. He prays for us each day and has left us in the care of the best Father we can have—our God, who watches over us day and night. *Thank you, Dad, for the wonderful gift of prayer!*

Reflection

Do you have a child or a parent that you need to entrust to God today?

Conversation with God

Lord, when the time comes that I know I cannot do what I want either for my child or for my parent, help me to remember to turn the reins over to You always.

God Made Them Male and Female

By Darlene Sala

---

*So God created man in his own image, in the image of
God he created him; male and female he created them.*

GENESIS 1:27

A wife prayed,

Dear Lord, I pray for wisdom to understand my husband,
Love to forgive him,
And patience for his moods.
Because, Lord, if I pray for strength,
I'll beat him to death. AMEN.

We laugh, but I'm afraid that's exactly how many a wife
would like to deal with the problems in her marriage.

Let me share a few thoughts about men that I think are very
important.

1. **Men have fragile egos.** They don't want us to know that,
   but it's true. Your husband may be an executive who
   directs the work of two thousand employees. But while
   he may never admit it, he's still uncertain of his abilities
   sometimes. At times his bluffing and braggadocio are
   merely a cover-up for a lack of self-confidence. Part of
   your contribution to your relationship is helping him
   feel better about himself.

2. **Your words have power to build him up or to pierce
   his heart.** Why are we so hesitant to compliment our

husbands and point out their strengths to them? Maybe we're afraid they'll become proud and egotistical. But actually, the more we encourage our husbands and help them to see their strengths, the better they'll feel about themselves—and us. Realize that his knowing that you think highly of him is very important to him.

3. **Sex is very important to your husband.** One of the reasons for this is that performance of any kind is very central to how he sees himself. So it follows that his ability to perform in bed is linked to his self-esteem.

4. **Remember, men and women resolve issues different ways.** Let's say you've just had an argument. How does he want to end the argument? With sex, of course. What you want is an apology, real repentance, and a promise that "It ain't gonna happen again!" Until you hear that, you are in no mood for intimacy. Yet, we need to recognize the needs of each other and the differences in each other in marriage.

My favorite verse when it comes to marriage is one we taught our kids as soon as they were able to memorize a Bible verse—Ephesians 4:32: "Be kind to one another, tenderhearted, forgiving one another, as God in Christ forgave you." Those three attitudes—kindness, tenderheartedness, and forgiveness—can make a tremendous difference in our marriages.

May God help us to offer grace during the challenging times!

Reflection _____

In marriage there is no room for selfishness.

Conversation with God _____

God, help me to show Your love during this hard time in my marriage.

The Love Your Spouse Challenge
By Luisa Reyes-Ampil

*Above all, love each other deeply,
because love covers over a multitude of sins.*
1 PETER 4:8 NIV

If you are on Facebook, a woman, and married, you probably have seen and/or been tagged for the *Love Your Spouse Challenge*. This is the popular seven-day event where you get to share old and new photos and write little posts announcing to your friends what's special about your spouse. It's actually fun to view the photos and read the messages!

Why was this *Love Your Spouse Challenge* created? Do couples who are experiencing drought in their marriages need a little shake-up to wake them up? And why does this challenge mostly appeal to women? What happened to the husbands, who also have the opportunity to profess their undying love for their spouses?

"Wives, submit to your own husbands, as to the Lord. . . . Husbands, love your wives, as Christ loved the church and gave himself up for her" (Ephesians 5:22, 25). Now this is the real *Love Your Spouse Challenge*! The apostle Paul stated *submission* as the wives' marital responsibility, while *loving* is that of the husbands. Why submission for the women and loving for the husbands?

A wife's submission to her husband is not a sign of weakness. In fact, it is a sign of love and courage. Jesus Himself submitted to God's plan and faced death on the cross. If He didn't love us, He wouldn't have gone through with the plan. If He didn't have courage, He would have walked away from the pain that He would have to endure.

A husband's love can be viewed in the same way. It takes a courageous man to go outside of his own need to nurture his wife. But a truly loving husband will do everything in his power to protect and care for his wife.

God's challenge to you, married ones, is that you do not take the spouse challenge for only seven days and later go scot-free. God's challenge is for you to show your spouses and the whole world that you will love one another unconditionally and be faithful to one another "for better, for worse, for richer, for poorer, in sickness and in health. . .till death do [you] part."

Reflection

How will you express your love to your spouse today? And then each day for the rest of your life?

Conversation with God

Stir in me and my spouse the love that we experienced at the beginning of our marriage. Fan it, Lord, so that the fire will not burn out within us.

Dark Days, Detours, and Dead Ends

For the times when you think you can't take even One. More. Step.

Grace in the Pain

By Bonnie Sala

Son though he was, he learned obedience from what
he suffered and, once made perfect, he became the
source of eternal salvation for all who obey him.
HEBREWS 5:8–9 NIV

Writer Ann Voskamp says, "There is not even one of us who hasn't lost something, who doesn't fear something, who doesn't ache with some unspoken pain."[70] There is pain, often great pain, in living, and the follower of Jesus Christ is not excluded from suffering this side of heaven.

However, suffering in the life of the believer and suffering outside of a life lived in relationship with God are two entirely different things. *Grace* is available to the believer, "a grace that holds you when everything is breaking down and falling apart—and whispers that everything is somehow breaking free and falling together."[71] Our God, "who gives life to the dead and calls into existence the things that do not exist" (Romans 4:17), is all about redemption, and that includes working good in our pain.

Jesus' wounds allowed for the redemption of our pain. God's own Son suffered! And the Word points out the result: "He learned obedience from what he suffered" (Hebrews 5:8 NIV), and that obedience required much pain. Bluntly put by Oswald

70 Ann Voskamp, *The Broken Way* (Grand Rapids, MI: Zondervan, 2016), 19.
71 Ibid., 20.

Chambers: "God's order is reached through pain and never in any other way."[72] If God's own Son went through the experience of learning obedience from suffering, I know He understands when I cry out to Him for strength to view my suffering as a pathway to good. But He also understands my cry for a way out.

In this world we " 'will have trouble' " (John 16:33 NIV), but the suffering of the believer is not fruitless and it comes with the promise that we *can* journey through: " 'My grace is all you need. My power works best in weakness' " (2 Corinthians 12:9 NLT). Have you experienced "handfuls of grace" in your life? Your car ran out of gas near the gas station? Your child broke her leg the day after the health insurance went into effect? Someone returned your lost wallet—with everything in it? If you begin to watch, you'll see that handful of grace in pain-filled valleys.

Reflection _____

What pain do you need to offer up to Jesus today?

Conversation with God _____

Thank You, Lord, that my pain is not without purpose because You promise to work redemptively right in the pain. Give me eyes to see Your ever-present grace in my life.

---

72 Chambers, *Shade of His Hand*, 59.

When God Doesn't Remove Suffering
By Darlene Sala

But [suffering] was to make us
rely not on ourselves but on God.
2 CORINTHIANS 1:9

You may have read the story or seen the movie of Joni Eareckson Tada, a young woman who became a quadriplegic at the age of seventeen as the result of a diving accident. As you can well imagine, when the accident happened she struggled with the part God had played in her resulting paralysis. Since He's all-powerful, why didn't He prevent the accident? Or why didn't He heal her? Her depression and pain eventually sent her on a search to understand how to deal with suffering.

People would remind her that Romans 8:28 says God works all things together for good—a verse often quoted to those who are going through painful, difficult-to-explain circumstances. Sometimes the verse is a comfort, but often what the person needed at that particular time was the knowledge not that good was going to come out of tragedy but that God was still there even through the pain—and He would always be there—and that He cares.

In Joni's book *When God Weeps*, she says while many prayed for her to be healed, she came to the realization that getting out of suffering is not the only solution. Suffering is a part of life. We paint ourselves into a corner when we insist that God must remove our suffering or we can never be happy again.

Joni says she has learned that a person's attitude toward suffering can make a tremendous difference in how they cope with painful circumstances that just don't go away—and she should know, having been paralyzed since 1967. "A Christian may not be able to rule their life situation," writes Joni, "but they can rule their hearts. It's wiser to subdue your heart to match your circumstances."[73]

The apostle Paul serves as our example. Through all his suffering, he could say, "I have learned in whatever situation I am to be content. . . . I can do all things through him who strengthens me" (Philippians 4:11, 13).

That may not be a lesson we would choose to learn, but God assures us He is sufficient in the most difficult of circumstances.

Reflection

"Reasons reach the head, but relationships reach the soul. It's the friendship of God reaching out to us throughout trials that draws the bottom line of suffering."—Joni Eareckson Tada[74]

Conversation with God

Lord, I want You to take away this pain I'm going through right now. But if You don't, I'm determined to learn to accept the pain and find happiness in You.

73 Joni Eareckson Tada and Steven Estes, *When God Weeps* (Grand Rapids, MI: Zondervan, 1997), 174.
74 Ibid., 126.

He Sees

By Bonnie Sala

*Then the people of Israel were convinced that the L*ORD*
had sent Moses and Aaron. When they heard that the
L*ORD *was concerned about them and had seen their
misery, they bowed down and worshiped.*

EXODUS 4:31 NLT

Bible teacher Beth Moore mentions in her Bible studies that she is
sometimes so overcome with God's powerful presence in her life
that she can only respond like the people of Israel, by dropping
right down on the floor (in private, that is) and worshipping Him.
I've had that experience myself, once in my life.

For many years, I had been in a difficult and eventually
abusive relationship. "You should leave." "You should stay," my
counselors and friends advised. The guidance from God's Word
wasn't explicit. The abuse became so intense that I despaired
of life. I just wanted things between me and Jesus to be clear.
Eventually, I stopped caring what anyone would say—I wanted
my life to be pleasing to God, and I wanted to go home to heaven
to be with Him. Now.

One desperate morning my Bible reading included Revelation
3:8 (NLT): " 'I know all the things you do, and I have opened a
door for you that no one can close. You have little strength, yet
you obeyed my word and did not deny me.' " *Interesting verse*,
I thought.

And then, the next day, "God saw my misery," as scripture says of the children of Israel in Exodus. Of course, He had seen it all along, but pain had its refining work to do in my life, and so it remained. On that summer morning, God led me to information that made it clear that I was released from the relationship. *"I know all the things you do, and I have opened a door for you that no one can close"* immediately came to my mind and I fell to my knees, for the presence of the living God was in the room.

In our deepest, most desperate pain, God is concerned about us. He sees our misery, and He allows it only as long as it is beneficial and necessary for producing the unperishable beauty He has selected to weave into our lives.

Reflection

Are you waiting for God to see your misery? Have you seen His concern for you?

Conversation with God

O God, I bow down and worship You because You do see my misery. You are concerned about me! If You have not yet chosen to remove a specific pain in my life, please give me an awareness of Your presence and speak through Your Word to me today.

Waters, Rivers, and Fires

By Darlene Sala

"Fear not, for I have redeemed you; I have called you by name, you are mine. When you pass through the waters, I will be with you; and through the rivers, they shall not overwhelm you; when you walk through fire you shall not be burned."

ISAIAH 43:1–2

Yesterday something happened in our family that made me cry. Oh, I know God is going to bring good out of the situation eventually, but it hurts just the same. I spent most of the night praying—not because I'm "spiritual," but for the very practical reason that I couldn't sleep.

Because I don't operate very well without sleep, I need some Bible verses to wrap my heart around today so I'll be able to sleep tonight. I've turned to Isaiah 43 because this chapter is entirely the words of the Lord—firsthand. You might want to read the whole chapter today.

Notice that in the opening verses God mentions three characteristics of trials in our lives. First, He talks about "waters," and I think He's talking about the depth of our problems. Then He refers to "rivers," which reminds us of the turbulence of our trials. Last, He speaks of "fires," and that reminds us of the intensity of our difficulties.

In verse 2, God uses the word *when*, not *if*. He doesn't say, *"If* you happen to go through deep waters or fast-paced rivers or scorching fire." He says, "*When* you pass through or walk through them." That means it should come as no surprise when difficulties crop up in our lives. We will always have problems to deal with. The good thing is that these situations are no surprise to God. Nor is any situation bigger than our God.

Are you, too, going through a time of difficulty? Let's review what God says He'll do for us in these situations:

1. When you pass through the waters, He will be with you.
2. The rivers will not overwhelm you.
3. You will not be burned in the fire.

These are God's promises. Did I neglect to mention that in verse 1, He says, "I have called you by name, you are mine"? How personal is that!

Reflection

"Trouble is one of God's great servants because it reminds us how much we continually need the Lord." —Jim Cymbala[75]

Conversation with God

Thank You, Lord, that You know me by name and I am Yours. Thank You for promising to be with me in the trials—they will not overwhelm me, nor will I be burned. I will think about that tonight as I go to sleep, knowing that You have everything under control.

75 Jim Cymbala, quoted in "68 Quotes about Trials," Christian Quotes, accessed October 31, 2016, https://www.christianquotes.info/quotes-by-topic/quotes-about-trials/#axzz4aC9Fia9S.

Broken for Life

By Bonnie Sala

*"Truly, truly, I say to you, unless a grain of wheat
falls into the earth and dies, it remains alone;
but if it dies, it bears much fruit."*

JOHN 12:24

The longer I live, the more painfully obvious it becomes: this world is broken and I am broken.

"The Bible paints for us a cover-to-cover portrait of a world that is disastrously broken, a world that does not function the way God intended,"[76] write Dave Harvey and Paul Gilbert. That brokenness exists not only in the world I see around me, but inside me. Our first inclination is to think that *something went wrong*, sometimes *very wrong*. We're broken and things aren't supposed to break. So, the believer says, "Well, God works all things for our good, beauty out of ashes" (Romans 8:28).

But what if there was more, much more, to our brokenness? What if God knew that we'd break, that creation would just break apart in defiance of Him, and so He *designed* life to burst forth out of that brokenness? A farmer's wife and daughter, Ann Voskamp says that *was* the plan. "The seed breaks to give us the wheat. The soil breaks to give us the crop, the sky breaks to give us the rain, the wheat breaks to give us the bread. And the

---

76 Harvey and Gilbert, *Letting Go*, 13.

bread breaks to give us the feast."[77]

Something radical, something God-designed, happens inside us in the breaking. "My dad told me this once," Voskamp explains. "For a seed to come fully into its own, it must become wholly undone. The shell must break open, its insides must come out and everything must change. If you didn't understand what life looks like, you might mistake it for complete destruction."[78]

Just as Jesus' brokenness made an eternity of friendship with God possible, our personal journeys of brokenness pave the way for us to embrace our fellow travelers, unafraid of their messes or of them seeing ours. After we are broken, after we relinquish ourselves to Him, it's then that we can truly be the "aroma of Christ to God among those who are being saved and among those who are perishing" (2 Corinthians 2:15).

Reflection

Have you lived out some of your own brokenness? Have you grown out of your own experience of coming "wholly undone" in ways that you *never* would have without your personal brokenness?

Conversation with God

Jesus, thank You for Your willingness to be broken for me so that new life can also come from the brokenness I experience in this life.

---

77 Voskamp, *The Broken Way*, 25.
78 Ibid., 26.

The God of All Comfort
By Darlene Sala

Praise be to the God and Father of our Lord Jesus Christ,
the Father of compassion and the God of all comfort.

2 CORINTHIANS 1:3 NIV

The day was my birthday, and no one could have had a nicer celebration as I enjoyed a beautiful tea with friends and family who are so dear. Truly it was a red-letter day.

The next day dawned bright and clear as well. But before that day ended, four disappointments and heartaches turned my emotional sky gray. My husband received word that the publisher he thought would give him a contract on his latest book had turned him down; our daughter learned she would face a financially devastating situation in court; a grandson was in trouble; and our niece had been informed by her doctor that she had stage four cancer. I felt as though I had been physically punched in the head—and the heart.

My mind searched scripture for comfort. I thought of Job, who likewise suffered four calamities in one day—but his were worse than mine. His servants plowing in the field were attacked by the Sabeans and killed. Lightning struck his sheep and the men caring for them, wiping out his flocks. Raiders stole all his camels and killed the caretakers. Then, as if that wasn't enough, a strong wind collapsed the house where Job's sons and daughters were eating together and they were all killed.

What was Job's response? "The LORD gave, and the LORD has taken away; blessed be the name of the LORD" (Job 1:21). What an amazing man!

When trouble comes, we often feel like no one understands what we're going through. Yet there is One who does—One who has been there. The apostle Paul, who himself experienced grief, loneliness, persecution, and yes, at times, even bouts of depression, described Him as the "God of all comfort." Here's what Paul said: "Praise be to the God and Father of our Lord Jesus Christ, the Father of compassion and the God of all comfort" (2 Corinthians 1:3 NIV). Then he adds a phrase I love: "who comforts us in all our troubles" (v. 4).

I am so glad the divine Comforter is my friend. And I'm so happy I can assure you that He wants to comfort you, too. It's who He is: "the Father of compassion and the God of all comfort."

Reflection

"Snuggle in God's arms. When you are hurting, when you feel lonely, left out. Let Him cradle you, comfort you, reassure you of His all-sufficient power and love."—Kay Arthur[79]

Conversation with God

Father of compassion and God of all comfort, enclose me in Your arms of love.

---

79 Kay Arthur, quoted in "47 Quotes about Comfort," Christian Quotes, accessed November 14, 2016, http://www.christianquotes.info/quotes-by-topic/quotes-about-comfort/?listpage=3&instance=2#participants-list-2.

On Dark Days

By Darlene Sala

For it is you who light my lamp;
the LORD my God lightens my darkness.
PSALM 18:28

When Harold and I were first married, we spent several months in Britain doing ministry. I remember visiting the coal mining region of England for the first time. The weather was cold and gloomy as we entered a little town whose buildings were darkened by the coal smoke. The laundry hanging on the clotheslines looked gray and dirty even though it had just been washed.

Turning to our host, my husband remarked, "I'd sure hate to live here. I'd think these folks would be depressed all the time." To his surprise, the man replied, "No, these are some of the happiest people in all England. They have learned to live above their circumstances." Amazing! We've never forgotten those words.

Maybe you are going through one of those dark periods of time when everything looks gray and discouraging. You wonder if you'll ever see the sunshine of happy days again. Try as you may, you don't seem to be able to rise above your circumstances.

Someone once said that "praise is the only shortcut to victory." And I think that is true. The apostle Paul wrote in 1 Thessalonians 5:18, "Give thanks in all circumstances; for this is the will of God in Christ Jesus for you." The hardest word for me in that verse is the word *all.* I can give thanks in some circumstances and, in fact, in most circumstances. But sometimes I hit a point where the pain is so bad that praise seems almost impossible. That's when I have to take up the shield of faith mentioned in Ephesians 6:16 "with which you can extinguish all the flaming darts of the evil one."

Put in plain words, I have to tell my emotions where to get off and then tell God that I do believe He is going to see me through the dark days and cause the light of His sunshine to shine once more in my heart.

The only way we can live above dark circumstances is to praise God that He is greater than our circumstances and will eventually bring us through the problems we face.

Reflection

"Though I fall, I will rise again. Though I sit in darkness, the LORD will be my light" (Micah 7:8 NLT).

Conversation with God

Right now, Lord, the sky is dismal and gray. I can't seem to break through the storm clouds that surround me. You are the only one who can lighten my darkness. I am going to praise You whether I feel like it or not. I'm going to trust You, for nothing is too hard for You.

What We Are, and What We Aren't

By Bonnie Sala

We are pressed on every side by troubles, but we are not crushed. We are perplexed, but not driven to despair. We are hunted down, but never abandoned by God. We get knocked down, but we are not destroyed.

2 CORINTHIANS 4:8–9 NLT

Have you noticed that somewhere in the back of your mind you think that the Christian life should inherently be a *better* life than that of a non-Christian? Perhaps when your Christian marriage faltered, your "Christian home–raised" child wandered, you disappointedly asked, *"Why?"*

Authors Dave Harvey and Paul Gilbert say this comes from "deterministic obedience," which they define as "the over-simplified belief that if I'm a Bible obeying spouse or a faithful parent, then my marriage will be faithful and my kids will be obedient. . .if you live in obedience, then God will reciprocate with immediate and discernable fruit."[80]

Yes, I did think this, if not consciously, then subconsciously. I should have paid more attention to Paul's speech on board a sinking ship when he told his fellow sailors, "I have faith in God that it will happen just as he told me," in Acts 27:25 (NIV), and here's the clincher in verse 26: "Nevertheless, we must run aground on some island." Yes, "running aground" is all a part of the human experience for each fallen human living on this broken planet. The apostle Paul, the poster child for the Christian living out the life of Christ in the real world (beaten, stoned, shipwrecked, you name it), has more for us.

I have two lists in my devotional journal that come from 2

---

80 Harvey and Gilbert, *Letting Go*, 58.

Corinthians 4:8–9: *What We Are* and *What We Aren't*. The first has certainly described my feelings on more than one occasion:

* Pressed on every side
* Perplexed
* Hunted down
* Knocked down

BUT, and that is the important word, here are the things the believer is *NOT*:

* Crushed
* Driven to despair
* Abandoned by God
* Destroyed

All of the things that we *are* are temporary. Yes, the pain is real. But it is temporary—we are not alone in it, it is at work for our good, and it will not be our undoing. This is the comfort of the believer. We have "this hope as an anchor for the soul, firm and secure" (Hebrews 6:19 NIV).

Reflection

Do you feel pressed, perplexed, hunted, and knocked down in some area of your life today?

Conversation with God

God, thank You that You are aware of the reality of my human condition! But thank You even more that You made it possible for me to have hope that is a firm, secure anchor for my soul!

God's Gift-Wrapped Grace
By Darlene Sala

*O Lord, you hear the desire of the afflicted; you will
strengthen their heart; you will incline your ear.*
PSALM 10:17

The man had a physical challenge—he was crippled and couldn't walk. The only way he knew to support himself was to beg at the temple gate in Jerusalem. You can read the story in the Bible in the book of Acts, chapter 3.

One morning the lame man awakened to what seemed like any other day. But on this day his life was to be forever changed. When the apostles Peter and John came to the temple that morning, he asked them for money. What they gave him, a gift of God's grace, could never be bought with all the money in the world. "I have no silver and gold," Peter told him, "but what I do have I give to you. In the name of Jesus Christ of Nazareth, rise up and walk" (Acts 3:6). The Bible says, "And leaping up, he stood and began to walk, and entered the temple with them, walking and leaping and praising God" (v. 8).

Peter gave him what money could not buy—wholeness and healing.

The lesson is twofold. Yes, God sometimes does heal physical problems supernaturally. That's exactly what God did for the crippled beggar. God has another kind of healing for us, and that is spiritual healing. He wants to break us out of the bondage that cripples us.

The beggar asked for money, figuring that would at least solve his problem of hunger. But money is not the answer to our deepest needs.

Money can buy

* A bed but not sleep
* Food to eat but not an appetite
* A house but not a home
* Medicine but not health
* A cross around your neck but not eternal life

No, money cannot solve all the challenges we have, but God can heal them. When we're crippled by life, God's great grace can result in our becoming strong, with joy in our hearts that makes us want to walk, jump, and praise God as the crippled man did. God's grace is sufficient to heal you either literally or to work miraculously in your life in such a way that you are not limited by the handicap. It's a gift of God's grace, His unmerited favor.

How do you find that healing? By coming to Him in all simplicity and committing your life fully to Him. Bring your deepest need to God. Let Him touch the area of your life that no one else can heal.

Reflection _____

Don't look at any problem as too big for God.

Conversation with God _____

Lord, I bring to You the deepest need of my life. Touch me and heal me as only You can.

Riding the Waves

By Bonnie Sala

Who shall separate us from the love of Christ?
Shall tribulation, or distress, or persecution, or famine,
or nakedness, or danger, or sword? . . . No, in all these things
we are more than conquerors through him who loved us.

ROMANS 8:35, 37

"The surf that distresses the ordinary swimmer produces in the surf-rider the super joy of going clean through it," wrote the Scottish evangelist Oswald Chambers. Now, I am a mother of two California surfers. (When they were growing up, we actually had a clothes dryer break down because the machine couldn't handle all the sand that refused to wash out of beach towels and trunks.) They aren't afraid of the surf. Big storm coming? Great! Waves that would terrify the average person were sources of big excitement around our house.

I'd rather have my life and my ocean dips both nice and calm. But Chambers says we should take a cue from surfers and "apply that to our own circumstances, these very things—tribulation, distress, persecution, produce in us super joy; they are not things to fight." Hmmm. I wouldn't exactly say that I've greeted tribulation, distress, and persecution with *super joy*. But Chambers bucks me up: "We are more than conquerors through Him *in* all things, not in spite of them, but in the midst of them. The saint never knows the joy of the Lord in spite of tribulation, but because of it."

We see in Romans 8 the order of things. Yes, verse 37 promises victory, but it's what's in verse 35 that makes the victory possible: nothing shall separate us from the love of God. *Nothing.* "Undaunted radiance is not built on anything passing, but on the love of God that nothing can alter. The experiences of life, terrible or monotonous, are impotent to touch the love of God, which is in Christ Jesus our Lord."[81]

This is love that I want to know and live in. And those big waves, that tribulation, distress, and persecution? I know they won't overwhelm me but that He, the Creator of heaven and earth, is in the swells with me. He is capable when I am not. David said, "With my God I can scale a wall" (Psalm 18:29 NIV), so I guess I can say, "With my God, I can ride the waves safely to shore!"

Reflection ─────────────────────────

Have you experienced the joy of going "clean through" a storm of life, of conquering through Him who loves you?

Conversation with God ─────────────────

I do want to know that "undaunted radiance" that comes from reliance on Your love! Teach me to conquer through Your love.

---

81 Oswald Chambers, "Undaunted Radiance," *My Utmost for His Highest*, March 7, 2016, accessed November 27, 2016, https://utmost.org/classic/undaunted-radiance-classic/.

Weak and Weary
By Darlene Sala

Likewise the Spirit helps us in our weakness. For we do not know what to pray for as we ought, but the Spirit himself intercedes for us with groanings too deep for words. And he who searches hearts knows what is the mind of the Spirit, because the Spirit intercedes for the saints according to the will of God.

ROMANS 8:26–27

Did you notice the word *weakness* in the first phrase of that scripture? What does that bring to your mind? Days when you're too tired to accomplish anything useful? A chronic illness you're dealing with day after day? Or perhaps times when you give in to temptation because you don't have the strength to resist?

My husband, who taught Greek, the language of the New Testament (let me tell you, it's great to live with a walking Bible concordance!), tells me *weakness* has three meanings.

> The first is physical illness.
> The second is moral failure.
> The third is weakness as opposed to strength.

In other words, *weakness* covers all three of those situations I mentioned above that you might be dealing with right now.

And how does the Spirit help us? Through prayer! Not just

our prayer—the kind that is composed of words. But the Holy Spirit prays for us with the kind of prayer that comes from the depth of your insides—too painful to be put into language. The Holy Spirit intercedes with God the Father for us with "groanings too deep for words." What's more, His intercession is always "according to the will of God."

So, when you're dealing with weakness of any kind, call without delay on His help. You may feel too helpless even to put your prayer in words, but know that the Holy Spirit understands. He can read your heart, and we have His promise that He will intercede for us with our heavenly Father.

How blessed we are!

Reflection

"When we pray for the Spirit's help. . .we will simply fall down at the Lord's feet in our weakness. There we will find the victory and power that comes from His love." —Andrew Murray[82]

Conversation with God

O Lord, You know that today I don't have the strength to do what needs to be done. I freely acknowledge my weakness. My need is so big that I don't even know how to put it into words. Help me as only You can.

---

82 Andrew Murray, quoted in "43 Quotes about Weakness," Christian Quotes, accessed October 29, 2016, http://www.christianquotes.info/quotes-by-topic/quotes-about-weakness/.

Our Ever-Present Help

By Bonnie Sala

God is our refuge and strength,
an ever-present help in trouble.
PSALM 46:1 NIV

The call came in the middle of the night—the one that you never want to get, that you prayed you'd never get. Anna had been sleeping fitfully that night, aware that her twenty-one-year-old son hadn't come in. She finally looked at her phone around 6:00 a.m. Yes, there was a voice mail message that had come in as she slept. She listened to the message; it was the voice of her son: *"Mom, I've been arrested for a DUI. I'm being taken to the sheriff's station."*

Now Anna, like me, has found herself in the role of single mom, living the life she never wanted, with no person next to her in bed that early morning, no one to share the immediate dismay that flooded her mind. I know what I would have done the instant I heard that phone message: I would have flipped out and called the first friend or family member who came to mind to help me think through what to do!

Not Anna. She and I had been praying for our sons, that God would use whatever means necessary to grow them up into the men of God we knew He wanted them to be. So what did Anna do? She went straight to prayer, praising God for this unwelcome turn of events, and then she picked up her Bible and did exactly what she does every morning: she "picked up her manna" that God had laid out for her in her morning Bible reading. *Then* she discussed the situation with others to help her think through her response.

I was stunned by her response. I thanked God for my friend who lived out her faith in front of me, for her complete trust in God, for the way she remembered who her ever-present help was. Hers was a vivid example of "seeking first" the kingdom, turning to our only Source of strength and power in time of need. Because middle-of-the-night calls come. We experience loss and disappointment and the unexpected on this journey called life. As I have heard Pastor Rick Warren say, "You have either just come through a crisis, are in one now, or will soon find yourself there." When the crisis comes, God is there, believing sister.

Reflection

How do you respond to crisis? By turning to the nearest person or to our God, our refuge and strength?

Conversation with God

God, thank You that You are ever present in our lives! Help me to remember this and turn instantly to You in times of need.

Treasure in a Dark Place

By Darlene Sala

[God] rewards those who earnestly seek him.
HEBREWS 11:6 NIV

In a little book called *Diamond Dust*,[83] I found an anonymous quote that caught my attention. Here it is: "If, in spite of all your tears and prayers, God has left you in a dark place, perhaps it's because He knows there are still treasures to be found there."

Those who work in mines know what darkness is—pitch-black darkness. Unless electricity has been brought to the mine, they're totally dependent on their miner's lamps to help them see anything at all. Yet, in that darkness exist valuable minerals, silver, gold—even diamonds.

So, too, in our lives there are precious discoveries to be found during the dark times. A few weeks after a friend of mine lost her son to suicide, someone asked her how she was doing. Her answer? "Devastated but not destroyed." In the dark God was revealing new insights into His love for her. New assurance that His grace is sufficient. New realization that in the deepest darkness He was still with her.

To find those valuable treasures, we must continue to seek God even when we cannot see how His hand is directing us. Hebrews 11:6 (NIV) says that "[God] rewards those who earnestly seek him." If we do, in Him we will find riches more valuable

83 *Diamond Dust*, December 26, 2008, stricker@netscorp.net.

than any gold or diamonds found on this earth.

Perhaps you are in a very dark place right now. Perhaps you've just lost the most precious person in your life. Or you've learned you have a physical condition for which there is no treatment. Or you've endured abuse by someone who should be treating you in a loving way. Don't give up. Continue to seek Him with all your heart, for God has promised, "You will seek me and find me, when you seek me with all your heart" (Jeremiah 29:13). You may want to write that verse down and carry it with you until the darkness lifts.

Who knows what jewels you will discover during this dark time? God rewards those who diligently seek Him even—or perhaps especially—in dark and difficult places.

Reflection _____

Trust God to help you find treasures in the darkness of your discouragement.

Conversation with God _____

I'm still here, Lord, in this dark place. Please give me a fresh realization that You are here with me and have not forgotten me. Give me courage to hang on.

Not the End of the Road

By Luisa Reyes-Ampil

"My grace is sufficient for you,
for my power is made perfect in weakness."

2 CORINTHIANS 12:9

My friends tell me my life story would be a perfect script for a soap! Many have followed my life challenges with tears, words of wisdom, and a lot of prayers.

I welcomed Jesus Christ in my life a month prior to my marriage falling apart, so I hit the ground running. I felt the uphill battle to stay on His track. The more determined I was to follow His road, the more I realized I had reason to hope.

In my small-group study of *The Grace Walk Experience*, this concept brought everything into perspective: "Problems in your life could be the best thing that could happen to you!"[84] Here are some truths I learned:

First, we sometimes need to go through brokenness. We may be prideful, thinking we are hot commodities. Some shake-up needs to happen so that we are not relying on ourselves but on our great God.

Second, we are not exempt from pain. God did not promise us a rose garden when we said yes to Him. In fact, we're supposed to prepare for trials and tribulations. But we do end up causing our own troubles at times—okay, most of the time—because of

---

84 Steve McVey, *The Grace Walk Experience* (Eugene, OR: Harvest House, 2004), 35–70.

wrong choices and simple disobedience. The moment we head back home to God, He can turn the painful experience into a joyful lesson—a beautiful testimony of His goodness and grace.

Third, we don't have to keep crying over the pain if we want to heal. It may hurt today, but the healing will come if you focus on God and not your difficulty.

I know we all want to avoid the words *problem* and *brokenness*. But if God's Word shows that they are *the best thing that could happen to you*, we just have to admit that we are definitely driven to our knees by the pain we experience. The path of pain does lead the believer to Jesus Christ. All you need to do is walk in it and reach out for His hand that offers comfort, peace, and wisdom. It's time to walk the path of victory.

Reflection —————————————————————

Are you experiencing grace in your struggle today?

Conversation with God ———————————————

Dear God, thank You that You will always walk with me and show me that my pain is not the end of the road!

Perseverance in Suffering

By Bonnie Sala

So then, those who suffer according to God's will should commit themselves to their faithful Creator and continue to do good.

1 PETER 4:19 NIV

"This is hard," I wrote in my journal one morning. "Faith is the substance of things hoped for, things not seen. I sure don't see any way out of this crisis. Ugh. I know I must reorient my gaze each and every morning off myself and onto the Creator of heaven and earth who loved me and gave Himself for me. It's just rugged, and my sin nature screams, 'No, no, no! I don't want to do this!' "

Have you ever felt like this? Have you been in a situation that was just so painful you couldn't possibly think of any way that this set of circumstances was ever going to turn into anything that could ever be considered *good*? You're sure you will not survive another day. You just can't *understand* the purpose of this pain!

In answer to this dilemma, Elisabeth Elliot quoted seventeenth-century French Jesuit Jean-Pierre de Caussade: "Perfection does not consist in understanding God's designs but in submitting to them. . . . They are God working in the soul to make it like Himself."[85] Submitting. Does that mean that I have to call this situation, this suffering, good? No. It means that I agree that I will continue today, or for the next hour, to

85 Elisabeth Elliot, "A Holy Aloneness," *The Elisabeth Elliot Newsletter* (March/April 1999).

trust myself to Jesus. To "continue to do good," as Peter put it.

I will do what I know I need to do; perseverance in suffering is a choice. I don't have to agree to suffer for a few more days, or until the end of the year, or even for the rest of my life. Just, yes, I will continue to do good. I choose to trust right now.

One of my favorite prayers in times like this is "Lord, make me willing to be made willing!" When we pray this way, we can be confident that He who began a good work in us will be faithful to complete it (Philippians 1:6). It's His work.

Reflection

When your life includes suffering, will you choose to trust Jesus and continue with Him?

Conversation with God

Lord Jesus, I trust myself to You right now and ask You for the power to continue on right now and believe that You will make a way for me.

Valleys

By Darlene Sala

*Even though I walk through the valley of the shadow
of death, I will fear no evil, for you are with me.*

PSALM 23:4

In life, we all like mountaintop experiences better than valleys. But the truth is that valleys are inevitable. Jesus didn't want us to be surprised by these difficult times, so just before He died on the cross, He warned us, "In the world you will have tribulation" (John 16:33). It's not a matter of *if*; it's a matter of *when*.

I'm sure you've noticed that you can't plan valleys or schedule them. I mean, have you ever had a flat tire or a root canal at a *good* time? But be encouraged that valleys are temporary; they do have an end. And they have a purpose. God will not waste our pain. The apostle Peter wrote, "Now for a little while, if necessary, you have been grieved by various trials, so that the tested genuineness of your faith—more precious than gold though it is tested by fire—may be found to result in praise and glory and honor at the revelation of Jesus Christ" (1 Peter 1:6–7).

Notice in our key verse that David, who was the one who wrote Psalm 23, refused to be filled with fear in the valleys because God was with him. Pastor, writer, and Bible teacher Andrew Murray once wrote,

*In times of trouble, God's trusting child may say,
FIRST: He brought me here; it is by His will I am in*

this strait place: in that will I rest. NEXT: He will keep me here in His love, and give me grace in this trial to behave as His child. THEN: He will make the trial a blessing, teaching me the lessons He intends me to learn. . . . LAST: In His good time He can bring me out again—how and when He knows.[86]

Then Murray encouraged us to say,

I am here—
1. By God's appointment.
2. In His keeping.
3. Under His training.
4. For His time.[87]

Thank You, Lord, for that truth!

Reflection

"For this light momentary affliction is preparing for us an eternal weight of glory beyond all comparison, as we look not to the things that are seen but to the things that are unseen" (2 Corinthians 4:17–18).

Conversation with God

Lord, help me to keep my eyes on You, not the situation I'm facing—not on my problem but on Your power. Thank You that You are with me and will never leave me. Hold my hand tightly. Amen.

86 Andrew Murray, "*In Times of Trouble God's Trusting Child May Say,*" Herald of His Coming, accessed November 4, 2016, http://www.heraldofhiscoming.com/Past%20 Issues/2015/February/in_times_of_trouble.htm.

87 Ibid.

As They Went

By Bonnie Sala

When he saw them he said to them, "Go and show yourselves
to the priests." And as they went they were cleansed.

LUKE 17:14

Often, when I have a serious problem, I just feel completely
stuck. What should I *do* about this? What will make everything
work out *perfectly*? I become paralyzed and miserable.

There were ten people in the Bible, in the book of Luke, with
a problem—a terrible problem that separated them from their
loved ones, from their homes: they had leprosy. They had to
stand at a distance as Jesus entered their village. All they could
do was cry out. And cry out they did: "Jesus, Master, have mercy
on us." (Luke 17:13). And Jesus heard them—the Bible says, "He
looked at them" (v. 14 NLT).

Now, a common element of Jesus' healing in so many of
the Gospel stories was touch. But Jesus didn't touch these
lepers. He didn't even say anything like, "Your faith has made
you well." He simply gave the lepers directions: "Go and show
yourselves to the priests." Did they think, *Wait…what? Jesus, the*
priests don't want to see us. We're unclean. How will seeing the
priests solve our problem? If they did hesitate or doubt, there's
no record of it. The next verse just says, "And as they went they
were cleansed." As they went. . .they simply obeyed even when
it didn't make much sense.

Getting back to my serious problem. God's Word tells me: "Don't worry about anything; instead, pray about everything. Tell God what you need, and thank him for all he has done" (Philippians 4:6 NLT). I once heard worry described as "spiritual adultery"—rather than going straight to God in prayer with my problems, I look elsewhere. I ask all my friends what they think I should do or I fret and fret, trying to think of some way I could possibly solve my dilemma myself.

Reflection

Do you feel paralyzed by a problem today? What is it that you know Jesus has already told you to do?

Conversation with God

Lord, I know You told me to come and be with You when I am "heavy laden" (Matthew 11:28), to ask You for wisdom (James 1:5), to wait for You (Psalm 27:14), and to submit to Your plan (Proverbs 3:5–6). I'm here, sitting in Your presence. I thank You for the perfect way You will make through the problems I face today, in Your perfect time.

Need Peace?

By Darlene Sala

Let the peace of Christ rule in your hearts.
Colossians 3:15

Have you noticed that when you see something in your home day after day, week after week, soon you fail to notice it? My husband experienced that when a brass plaque appeared on his desk adjacent to his computer monitor, sitting snugly against the wall. The message? A verse from Paul's letter to the Colossians that reads: "Let the peace of Christ rule in your hearts. . . . And be thankful."

Wondering where it had come from, Harold picked it up and placed it in a prominent place. Then a few days later, he glanced at the wall and noticed that a wooden base slightly larger than the brass plaque with some dried glue on it was hanging from a nail. He realized the brass plate had simply fallen from the plaque and landed where it got his attention.

He began focusing on the message on the plaque: "Let the peace of Christ rule in your hearts," said Paul. No, that isn't something that takes place automatically, but something you allow to happen—as if peace is knocking at the door of your life and you have barricaded the door with worries and concerns, piling the furniture of self-striving and your plans and goals against the door as though peace were an intruder.

God's peace can rule in your heart only as you allow the

Prince of Peace to take control. What convicted Harold of his lapse is that right then there were a lot of things on his plate that he felt were consistent with what God wanted done, but when he is interrupted or things don't quite come together as quickly as he would like them to, he admits that like most of us, he gets impatient and, yes, irritated.

Who is really in control? The Lord, who calmed the storm that threatened the disciples' fishing boat? Or do we allow the storm to trouble us, forgetting that His presence in the boat is far more important than the storm that has darkened the sky?

I don't know if God caused the brass plaque to drop off the wooden base, but I do know it got Harold's attention and reproved him for allowing stuff that is inconsequential and unimportant to rob him of God's peace.

Yes, letting Christ's peace rule our hearts is our decision, something we choose to do. Think about it.

Reflection

"Peace is belief that exhales."—Ann Voskamp[88]

Conversation with God

Lord, I admit that when storms come in my life, they very quickly get my attention. Help me to remember You are with me in the storm. Rule my heart with Your peace.

---

88 Ann Voskamp, Twitter, November 21, 2013, accessed August 8, 2016, https://twitter .com/annvoskamp/status/403699832990093312.

Walk It Out

A long obedience in the
same direction gets us there

Walking It Out

By Bonnie Sala

---

*So I say, walk by the Spirit, and you
will not gratify the desires of the flesh.*
GALATIANS 5:16 NIV

"Walking by the Spirit" has always made me think of a super-spiritual, tranquil state. I imagined a condition where I would be on Holy Spirit–powered autopilot. But sometimes different versions of scripture help by expressing God's truth with slightly different words. The New Living Translation puts Galatians 5:25 this way: "Since we are living by the Spirit, let us *follow the Spirit's leading* in every part of our lives," and the English Standard Version says: "If we live by the Spirit, let us also *keep in step with* the Spirit" (emphasis added).

This makes it a little clearer for me, because I can relate to the concept of following or walking alongside someone. I think of the inexperienced runner preparing for a race. Often a veteran racer will run alongside the new runner, setting the pace necessary for the "newbie" to make it across the finish line in the desired amount of time. Left to pace herself, to judge her energy on her own, the novice might head out too fast and be unable to finish the course.

Now God knows what He created me to accomplish and the speed at which I am to do it. As anyone close to me knows, I was born with a certain, shall we say, energy level. (The doctor told my mom to "get me outdoors a lot" after I jumped through three crib mattresses.) So, heading out of the gates of my adult life, I was pretty sure I knew what needed to be done (yes, that would be pride) and when it needed to be done. . .now (yes, impatience).

And guess what? Walking by my power didn't work out very well. Eventually, I came closer to author Rachel Devenish Ford's question: "Is walking my life out more a matter of stumbling from situation to situation, asking God to create stability in my heart, to keep me standing by the sheer strength of who he is for me?"[89]

Yes, the Spirit is the stability giver of my life. His are the "unforced rhythms of grace" (Matthew 11:28–30 MSG). I've learned the Spirit's steps aren't rushed; keeping in step with Him requires quiet space in my life and the Word.

Reflection _____

Have you discovered how to follow or keep in step with the Holy Spirit on a daily basis?

Conversation with God _____

Holy Spirit, please teach me Your unforced rhythms of grace. Help me to learn what life looks like when I am in step with You.

---

89 Rachel Devenish Ford, *Trees Tall as Mountains: The Journey Mama Writings* (Small Seed Press, 2013), Kindle edition, chap.

Wise Ants

By Luisa Reyes-Ampil

Go to the ant, you sluggard;
consider its ways and be wise!
PROVERBS 6:6 NIV

I once read a Vanguard Investment Funds print ad that read: "SIMPLE TRUTH: . . .stay the course. Building wealth slowly is better than building it fast, then losing it fast." And to illustrate this, the ad showed two investment models using stacked rocks: the "build wealth slowly" model displayed a series of rock piles that gradually increased in size, whereas the "chasing trends" model was illustrated by a random mixture of big and small stacks of rocks. The second model showed how disastrous it can be to go after risky ventures. The ad made me think of a couple I know who invested in a get-rich-quick scam and lost everything because they weren't content to build slowly.

"Go to the ant, you sluggard; consider its ways and be wise!" says Proverbs 6:6 (NIV). This verse makes me laugh and think long and hard at the same time. Here is a tiny insect that God made as an example of hard work. We don't like ants and use bug spray or step on them to kill them. But do you know that they are also fascinating to watch when they are at work gathering food? I remember telling my niece Ely one time to break off a piece from her cookie to use as ant bait. We waited until we saw a couple of ants scout it and begin carrying portions of the cookie back to their home—a little at a time—just like slowly stacking the rocks of your "build wealth slowly" investment!

A few of us may have the opportunity to get rich quick and stay that way for life. Most of us, though, need to work. The bottom line is what we do with what we have. Are we living beyond our means? If so, we need to quit that strategy and learn how to budget! Are we using a portion of our treasure to enable the work of Christ? If so, well and good! It's always a wonderful thing when you invest in kingdom work for God.

Saving for rainy days? If not, you may have to learn a great lesson from our friend the ant: "[storing] its provisions in summer and [gathering] its food at harvest" to prepare for the coming lean days (Proverbs 6:8 NIV).

Reflection

What lifestyle changes do you need to make for you to "gather more harvest"?

Conversation with God

Dear God, teach me to manage what You have blessed me with. Help me to understand that everything belongs to You so I can use resources wisely and invest in kingdom work.

Judge Not
By Luisa Reyes-Ampil

*"Do not judge by appearances,
but judge with right judgment."*

JOHN 7:24

We often make quick judgments based on what we see. I was in San Antonio, Texas, with some friends, walking around the downtown area. We saw African-American and Mexican teenagers everywhere—in gangster-looking outfits. Elsa, my friend, and I immediately started thinking of safety and made sure our purses were secure.

On our return flight to California, we sat next to an elderly Caucasian lady. She gave us a quick look-see and decided we were not "white" like her (Elsa and I are Filipinas)—exactly like what we had done! The lady hung her purse around her neck and didn't glance our way thereafter. Ouch! *What's wrong with you, lady?*

While in flight, we noticed the lady rummaging through her purse with difficulty. Elsa offered help and was snubbed. Fifteen minutes before landing in Houston, the lady was sweating heavily and still frantically searching for something. Elsa noticed her insulin syringes. A diabetic herself, Elsa immediately alerted me, and I grabbed my Snickers bar to offer to her. We called the flight attendant to let him know what was going on. The flight attendant brought orange juice and radioed ahead for medical help.

In the end, Elsa and I stayed with seventy-seven-year-old Thelma DeMarco, sitting with her at the Houston airport waiting area until the paramedics arrived to take her to the hospital. She was teary-eyed as we calmed her down and bought her snacks, refusing her money as payment. We learned that she had suffered two strokes, causing her right side to be semiparalyzed, and she was moving to a nursing home to be closer to her daughter. We felt sad that she had to fly the distance alone in her condition and now had to be taken to the hospital. We prayed for her and hugged her as we left to catch our own flight home.

God help us as we live out our prejudices! When all we can see is someone's physical appearance or the color of their skin, we will never be able to do what the Lord wants us to do. Had we chosen to ignore Thelma after she treated us coolly in the beginning, circumstances could have been very serious.

Reflection

Have you ever been judged unfairly or judged someone else on their appearance?

Conversation with God

Lord, I know that I judge people wrongly at times. Help me to step outside of my culture and life experiences and see myself and others with Your eyes. Teach me to love unconditionally.

You Are the Strategy!
By Bonnie Sala

*How beautiful on the mountains are the feet of the messenger
who brings good news, the good news of peace and salvation,
the news that the God of Israel reigns!*

ISAIAH 52:7 NLT

Anuja Lal is a vibrant woman with dark, soft hair, dressed in a bright yellow Nepalese pantsuit. Lal and her husband, Deepak, plant churches in Nepal and Northern India, and she empowers women through vocational training and microenterprise. She stands in front of a roomful of women (and a few men) in Southern California—mission workers, strategists, and women from church missions committees—and reminds them of something they've forgotten: "We women are pioneers!"[90] Now it seems like a long time ago that women were riding in covered wagons and homesteading in the western United States or even settling new villages in Asia or anywhere else in the world!

But Lal isn't talking about pioneering in this world but in the *kingdom of God*. She's talking about carrying out what we call the Great Commission of Matthew 28:19–20: " 'Go therefore and make disciples of all nations, baptizing them in the name of the Father and of the Son and of the Holy Spirit, teaching them to observe all that I have commanded you.' "

---

90 Anuja Lal, "Women *AS* Strategy," (lecture, Finishing the Task Conference, Lake Forest, CA, December 7, 2016).

"We are natural networkers!" Lal says exuberantly. "We talk about our children, our marriages, our work. Women are about relationship, and we much more readily invite each other into our homes and into our lives than men do." Lal says she finds that "wherever you go in the world, women are interested in spiritual things. They generally want to know about God."[91] (You're reading this devotional, aren't you?) When the Church is looking for a "strategy" for sharing the hope of Christ, Lal says, *we are it!* "Today's world is all about one-to-one dialogue, not monologue. The days of standing on street corners and preaching are long gone," Lal explains.

Dialogue? We can do that!

Here's how it works: "Tell your story, tell God's story, and tell how God's story and your story came together."[92] That's it. You don't need to memorize any script, go to Bible school, or understand theological terms. Your story, God's story, and a conversation.

Reflection

Have you ever stopped to think about your story and where God's story and yours came together?

Conversation with God

Help me to grasp that You've already perfectly equipped me to share the hope that is within me, and show me who is longing to talk about You.

91 Ibid.
92 Ibid.

Want Ad

By Luisa Reyes-Ampil

And the word of God continued to increase, and the number of the disciples multiplied greatly in Jerusalem, and a great many of the priests became obedient to the faith.

ACTS 6:7

Job Description: A fellowship is seeking seven outstanding men for a unique task. Must be reputable, spiritual, and wise.

This "want ad" came about during the rapid growth of the early church—an increase in the thousands as people recognized Jesus of Nazareth as the Messiah. The Hellenists (Greeks) were complaining against the Hebrews because their widows were being overlooked in the daily distribution of food. The twelve apostles were busy with their preaching and couldn't wait on tables as well.

The book of Acts tells about the need to select seven men to wait on tables—to make sure that no one was left out in the food distribution. Qualifications: "men of good repute, full of the Spirit and of wisdom" (6:3). In any industry today, education and previous experience will probably top the job requirements to minimize training on the employer's part. But not for *this* unique and special fellowship. They needed men who were honest because of the Holy Spirit's work in their own lives even when no one would be supervising.

I answered a similar "want ad" when Dr. Harold Sala offered

me a ministry position at Guidelines International Ministries. I was working then as a director of catering at a five-star hotel. God was speaking to my heart and I couldn't say no. I didn't even ask for his salary offer. I just gave him a start date!

And while waiting to get my work visa, the lawyer set down my lengthy résumé and asked me, "What else will you be bringing to the table for this ministry work?"

You see, we often overlook the fact that people who serve others should first have a real heart for God and His work. It is difficult to attend to differing needs, meet requests, and answer complaints and still have a smile on your face, then do it all over again the next day. The "ministry of relief" definitely is not the job for any fainthearted Jesus follower!

Reflection

Do you know where and how you can serve people in your life?

Conversation with God

Lord, give me a cheerful heart as You send me where You see me fit to serve. Help me to always see Your face in the faces of the people I serve.

Life at Its Best

By Darlene Sala

May the God of hope fill you with all joy and peace in believing,
so that by the power of the Holy Spirit you may abound in hope.
ROMANS 15:13

In his book *Senior Moments*, Willard Spiegelman expressed a very sad view on life: "We come into the world alone, with a cry," he reminds us. "We exit alone, to confront the final eternal silence. The fun, all the pleasure and adventure, lies in between."[93]

How sad! All you have, Spiegelman says, is the enjoyment you can extract from the seventy to ninety years you're alive on this earth. And then it's over.

Contrast that life view with the apostle Paul's, who said, "For I consider that the sufferings of this present time are not worth comparing with the glory that is to be revealed to us" (Romans 8:18).

In the Bible, there is no mention of a "final eternal silence." But to those who put their faith in Him, Jesus says, "Let not your hearts be troubled.... In my Father's house are many rooms. If it were not so, would I have told you that I go to prepare a place for you? And if I go and prepare a place for you, I will come again and will take you to myself, that where I am you may be also" (John 14:1–3). What makes the difference in these two attitudes—hopelessness versus hope—is a relationship with Jesus Christ.

---

93 Quoted by Gerard Helferich in "Life in the Fourth Quarter," *Wall Street Journal*, September 3–4, 2016, C7.

Some Bible scholars point out that Jesus talked more about hell than He did about heaven. Paul says that when Jesus returns to earth, those who do not know God and do not obey the Gospel of our Lord Jesus will suffer "the punishment of eternal destruction, away from the presence of the Lord and from the glory of his might" (2 Thessalonians 1:9). What a tragedy that would be!

Right now make sure that your eternal future is secure—that you have placed your faith in Jesus and put your life into His hands. When you know Him, you have the very best this life can offer—and then all eternity to enjoy His presence. How can you lose?

Reflection

Take a few minutes to read 1 Corinthians 15 to encourage yourself that death has no sting, the grave has no victory for those who trust in Jesus. The best is yet to come.

Conversation with God

Dear Lord, thank You for the hope of eternity with You. What joy that brings to my heart when life is hard!

The Earring
By Luisa Reyes-Ampil

"There is joy before the angels of
God over one sinner who repents."
LUKE 15:10

I was in the tiny confines of my cabin's bathroom getting ready to go ashore when the cruise ship rolled hard over a wave, causing one of my dangling earrings to fly off and drop straight down the sink drain. I stood in shock! I loved my five-dollar one-of-a-kind earrings that I had bought from a young artist while I was in Ecuador on a mission trip. So I called the steward—thankfully, a fellow Filipino—and asked for help. He promised to have the sink trap opened. Returning from the tour, I was so happy to see my pair of earrings laid out on my dresser that I gave him a tip!

In Luke chapter 15, we read of three parables with the same theme: lost and found. The first one is the lost sheep among a hundred that the owner searched for until found. The second is of a woman who lost one of her silver coins; she lit a lamp, swept the house, and sought diligently until it was found. The last story is of the prodigal son, who claimed his inheritance from his father, went away to a far country, and squandered his money on an unhealthy lifestyle. Finding himself in need, he eventually worked feeding pigs. He longed to eat what the pigs had, but at the same time he remembered how his father's servants had more. So he went back home, asked for his father's forgiveness, and was reinstated as a rightful son. Note that at the end of each parable was the "big find" that brought tremendous joy to the searchers, followed by rejoicing and celebration. Lost, but now found!

Each believer knows of someone who has yet to receive the free gift of salvation offered by Jesus Christ. I am sure that you are knocking on heaven's door on that loved one's behalf. Or you may have met someone in crisis and you know there is nothing else except Christ that will make a difference. It will not only be you whose heart will be gladdened, but also God and His angels when that big day comes! Don't give up until the lost is found!

Reflection

Who do you want to pray for to receive God's salvation today?

Conversation with God

Lord, I come before You to ask that You soften the heart of _____, that he/she will be able to receive Your gift of salvation and eternal life. Thank You for Your untiring patience toward the lost and unconditional love to find them.

Giving Your Body to God
By Darlene Sala

I appeal to you therefore, brothers, by the mercies of God,
to present your bodies as a living sacrifice.
ROMANS 12:1

Though my dad was in pubic ministry for more than seventy years, my mom hardly ever spoke to groups in public. That's why after she passed away, I was so happy to find some rare speaking notes of hers. She brought a message based on Romans 12:1, where the apostle Paul writes, "I appeal to you therefore, brothers, by the mercies of God, to present your bodies as a living sacrifice." The verse goes on to say that this sacrifice is an act of "spiritual worship." If that concept seems hard for you to grasp, perhaps the King James Version adds meaning for you, calling this our "reasonable service"—reasonable in light of all that God has done for us.

She noted that it was our bodies God asked for, not just our minds. We should pick our bodies up, she said, and offer them to God, making them do the work He has given us to do. Just serving the Lord with our minds will not get the job done.

She noted that sometimes when people haven't attended an event in person, they will say, "Well, I was there with you in spirit." There's not much inspiration, however, from a bunch of spirits—and not much accomplished. But the spirit accompanied by a body makes a great impression for the Lord. It's easy to present your soul to the Lord—you can't see it or control it. Presenting your body to God, however, involves time, effort, discipline, and unselfishness.

You're probably familiar with Psalm 103:1, which says, "Bless the LORD, O my soul, and all that is within me, bless his holy name." My dad used to say that sometimes he didn't feel like blessing the Lord. In those times he humorously told that he would stand his soul up in the corner and *make* it bless the Lord, regardless of how he felt! Sometimes we have to exercise the same discipline with our bodies.

Someday we'll know that everything we've done here on earth for the Lord was well worth the effort. So today pick up your body, so to speak, present it to the Lord for whatever purpose He has, and make it do the work He has given you to do.

Reflection

God sees our motives as well as our actions. He knows when we make the effort to do something difficult.

Conversation with God

Right now, Lord, I want to present my body to You to be used for Your eternal purpose—today.

Fruit-Bearing

By Luisa Reyes-Ampil

Do not neglect to do good and to share what you have,
for such sacrifices are pleasing to God.

HEBREWS 13:16

I enjoy reading newsletters from missionaries all over the world. One that I definitely print out and share with others comes from Pami Ellis of Shalom Birthing Center in Antipolo, Philippines.

A beautiful American nurse, Pami was raised as a missionary kid in the Philippines and returned to the country to be a missionary herself. Pami, along with the Shalom team, provides pre- and postnatal health care and the Gospel to impoverished women and their families. She has been bearing fruit not only at the center but also beyond its walls for years.

But years before, when Pami was a college freshman in a California university, she had wanted to get a free pass to a concert, so she volunteered with a friend at the Compassion International booth. As she worked the booth of this child sponsorship organization, she shuffled through the picture cards of children available for sponsorship, looking for a child from the Philippines that she could sponsor. Pami selected one at random and ended up sponsoring a girl named Princess from the Philippine city of Cebu.

Pami and Princess exchanged letters and photos over the years. In the beginning, it was Princess's mom writing until

Princess learned to write on her own. Pami enjoyed reading about the youth camps and church events. She prayed fervently for Princess as she sensed Princess's home life was tough.

Compassion International informed her years later of Princess's acceptance to a competitive program called Leadership Development Program. Pami couldn't afford a university sponsorship for Princess this time, so she prayed for someone to fill in for her. Pami and Princess lost touch.

Then in 2016 Pami's friend, who works at Compassion International, was working with some of their program's graduates and came across Princess's graduation speech. Princess had included Pami's name as one of her sponsors. Although Pami wasn't able to attend Princess's graduation, she surprised her with a recorded video message.

Pami was a missionary kid who didn't grow up with a lot of money. However, she did learn the heart of God at an early age and put into motion God's command "to do good and share" what she had. Her obedience bore fruit in the life of a girl named Princess!

Reflection

Are you willing to share what you have with someone else?

Conversation with God

Teach me, Lord, to step out in faith and make a difference in someone today by sharing what You have given to me!

"I Shoulda..."

By Darlene Sala

*"You keep him in perfect peace whose mind
is stayed on you, because he trusts in you."*
ISAIAH 26:3

Her name is the Shoulda Finger-Pointer, and she comes around to spoil your peace of mind, especially after any kind of social event. She's the little voice inside that robs us of peace and joy when she makes us shake our fingers at ourselves and say, "You *should* have done more." Or, "You *should* have done it differently." Or even something as frivolous as "You *should* have known better than to wear *that* dress tonight."

My friend Joanie Feuerstein told me she knows the Shoulda Finger-Pointer quite well. She says, "This one gets real talkative when you've finally made it to bed after a big event, especially if you were in charge of it. Yak-yak-yak half the night! Yes, I know her quite well," Joanie moans. Oh, and let me warn you: she picks a time when you're really tired to pull this one.

As I said, one of the worst things the Shoulda Finger-Pointer does is to rob us of peace and joy. She centers our attention on ourselves instead of letting us put past events in God's hands and leave the results to Him. You can't change the past—it's over, and what's done is done. So what should you do?

When this happens to me, I come back to God's promise in Isaiah 26:3 that says, " 'You keep him in perfect peace whose mind is stayed on you, because he trusts in you.' " You'd think I'd have that one down pat by now, but I don't. Over and over I have to put that verse into practice by centering my thoughts on the Lord, not on other people's opinions.

So next time the Shoulda Finger-Pointer gives you trouble, tell her to get lost! Begin to praise God for all the blessings of your day—one by one. As you do, His peace and joy will flood your heart.

Reflection

Thanking God for His blessings sends the Shoulda Finger-Pointer running. What good things has God done for you in the past twenty-four hours?

Conversation with God

Lord, help me today to truly center my thoughts on You, not me.

Tall Tales & Lying Lips

By Luisa Reyes-Ampil

*Therefore, having put away falsehood, let each one of you speak
the truth with his neighbor, for we are members one of another.*
Ephesians 4:25

My three-year-old niece Mikaela was entertaining us with her
stuffed Mickey Mouse when she started vigorously scratching
her arm. I asked if she had been bitten by an ant, and she said,
"No! Lexi put detergent on my arm so I have been itching."
Concerned, I asked her mom if this was true. "You know what
stories these two cook up." Mikaela's sister Lexi is two years old;
and between the two siblings, they are known for their escapades.

We might put a toddler's tall tale in the same category as
"stretching the facts." For instance, when we are describing a
funny event that happened to us, sometimes isn't it so tempting
to stretch the facts to make the story even funnier? Or when
something goes wrong, we find it easy to gloss over small details
that reveal the part we played in the situation.

God is crystal clear on lying: "The LORD detests lying lips,
but he delights in those who tell the truth" (Proverbs 12:22 NLT).
"But is it ever right to tell a lie?" Pastor John Piper was asked.
His answer: "It is possible to be a person who never intentionally
lies and yet be a hardened sinner, living in darkness and cut off
from Christ in unbelief; and it is possible to be a person who
fears the Lord, walks by faith, and yet feel constrained in extreme,

life-threatening situations to oppose evil by lying intentionally."[94]

As Christians, lying is a behavior that is a part of our "old natures"—we are inclined to lie because the old nature is enslaved to deceitful desires. Usually they're desires based on greed or fear. Ephesians 4:22 warns us to "put off" our old natures so that we can then speak truth! The secret to being able to do this is in "renewing our minds" with the promises of God (Romans 12:2). He speaks to our greed and fear all through His Word.

God can help us watch our words each time we open our mouths!

Reflection

Do you struggle with lying of some sort or another?

Conversation with God

God, "set a guard, O LORD, over my mouth; keep watch over the door of my lips!" (Psalm 141:3).

---

94 John Piper, "Speak Truth with Your Neighbor," Desiring God, September 28, 1986, accessed December 26, 2016, http://www.desiringgod.org/messages/speak-truth-with-your-neighbor.

Stop!
By Luisa Reyes-Ampil

Don't have anything to do with foolish and stupid arguments,
because you know they produce quarrels.
2 TIMOTHY 2:23 NIV

You are in a room with friends. One throws out a question, a challenging one. Several take the bait and comment—they can't stand not contributing. A few decide to stay noncommittal. Which one are you in that group? If I look at myself in the mirror while in this company, I can already see my widening eyes, raised eyebrows, and racing mind. Go ahead and guess which group I belong to!

We are sometimes presented with a question that can only be answered two ways—what we want to hear and what we don't want to hear. When people in a group share the same thoughts, there is no argument. Closed book. Happy ending. Everyone gets along. But when someone offers a view different from what we have in mind, we sometimes cannot resist a rebuttal. The situation often snowballs to a point of confusion where we can't see eye to eye about anything. Some get offended and leave with hurt feelings. The end result: a quarrel over an issue that probably was unimportant to begin with.

Why do we get trapped into arguments? Honestly put, we are prideful people! We don't want anyone to get the better of us. We cannot accept the fact that we can be wrong at times or our thinking can be off tangent on some issues. We rant and rave and fight so we can be right—even if we are wrong!

As Christians, we are called to pursue righteousness, faith, love, and peace. And all these are hard to have if we are going under our own power. Most of us know that we should avoid nonedifying situations—in fact, anything contradictory to what the Bible says.

Instead of spending time arguing and bickering, why not think of ways that will encourage, uplift, and promote healthy relationships? After all, it isn't worth it to waste our time and energy to be at odds with someone we know and love. So stop and think twice about what the apostle Paul said, "that we may be mutually encouraged by each other's faith, both yours and mine" (Romans 1:12).

Reflection

Which is more important—to win an argument that is getting out of hand or to bring a peaceful resolution?

Conversation with God

I want to be a channel of Your peace, dear Lord. In moments when I want to say something that will stir the pot, give me Your Word so I can speak with love.

Still Learning
By Darlene Sala

"Take my yoke upon you, and learn from me."
MATTHEW 11:29

"Learn from me," Jesus said.

Learn? I think I have the basics of the Christian life down pretty well, you may be thinking. *I've been a believer now for many years. Is there still more to learn?*

Because some of us know a lot of facts about the Bible, and we know a libraryful of Bible stories, and we know the basic doctrines of the faith, we think there's probably not much more to learn. Isn't it easy to fall into that trap!

The phrase "learn from me" comes from Matthew 11:29, where Jesus said, "Take my yoke upon you, and learn from me." The picture Jesus used is, of course, a familiar one to farmers in parts of the world where there are no tractors but only a wooden bar harnessing two oxen together so they can plow the fields together. If we are "harnessed" to Jesus, that means that we learn from Him "on the job"—every day living life together with Him walking alongside us.

But think again of *who* offers to teach us in this very personal way—the very Son of God. It's one thing to study a book, even the Bible. It's quite another to have the author, the Lord Jesus, walk alongside us day by day teaching us how we should live. Imagine being in a classroom where Einstein himself taught you the theory of relativity. Jesus' offer, however, is even better than that. He offers not classroom lecturing but individual on-the-job tutoring.

The Lord teaches us by showing us how to apply scripture to our lives in a practical way. Note these verses: "You guide me with your counsel" (Psalm 73:24). "The LORD will guide you continually" (Isaiah 58:11). "Lead me in your truth and teach me, for you are the God of my salvation" (Psalm 25:5). "Teach me to do your will, for you are my God! Let your good Spirit lead me on level ground!" (Psalm 143:10).

I like the way *The Message* paraphrase puts it: " 'Walk with me and work with me—watch how I do it. Learn the unforced rhythms of grace. I won't lay anything heavy or ill-fitting on you.' " We are privileged that Jesus offers to teach us personally. Yes, Lord, I want to be yoked to You and to learn from You every single day.

Reflection

There's always more to learn from Jesus. Are you listening?

Conversation with God

Teach me, Lord, as this day I walk step by step yoked together with You.

On a Diet

By Luisa Reyes-Ampil

"It is written, 'Man shall not live by bread alone,
but by every word that comes from the mouth of God.'"
MATTHEW 4:4

I have struggled with weight issues since I was a kid—I was one of those "bouncing" babies that tipped the scale at over 8.5 pounds at birth. My poor mom has listened to all my wailing over what I should do to reduce this and that part of my body all my life.

As an adult I have done all sorts of exercises—aerobics, Zumba, Hot Hula, weights. I have also tried many kinds of diets—vitamin supplements only, apples and tuna for all meals, and even a nutritionist-controlled diet. But after all these "healthy" processes, the weight returns as well as the simple joys of normal life.

Thank God that there is one food that I have been gorging on for many years now that has only served to grow the best part of me: my spirit! Jesus said, "It is written, 'Man shall not live by bread alone, but by every word that comes from the mouth of God'" (Matthew 4:4). Let me tell you more about this diet plan.

First, there is no fee to have *this* personal nutritionist and trainer. You don't need to work around His schedule, for He is always available. To join, all you need to do is believe and confess Jesus (Romans 10:10). Second, this diet is not limited to one meal a day. It is an "eat as much as you can at any time of the day any day for free" plan! You can pile your plate high. Third, just like those fat-burner pills or creams that claim to do some work even when you're not doing anything, this diet burns away your earthly desires and trims your "poor me" image.

Jesus also provides the following benefits with this special diet:

1. He shows us the path to take. We can avoid the sweet temptations along the way!
2. He provides wisdom. It's easy to pick a munchie from His basket of goodies!
3. He brings us satisfaction. We are always full—never hungry!
4. He gives us peace. We won't ever feel guilt no matter how much we take in!

So if you are looking for the best diet to have, *this is it*!

Reflection

Just think how great it is that God provides the most spiritually satisfying meal plan!

Conversation with God

Praise You, God, for Your Word gives ultimate satisfaction every time we partake of it!

Experiencing Sensory Overload?
By Darlene Sala

Take every thought captive to obey Christ.
2 CORINTHIANS 10:5

When I crawl in bed at night, sometimes my mind doesn't want to turn off—like a computer that has too many files open at the same time. The houseguests who are coming this weekend, the latest terrible shooting on the news, packing for an upcoming trip, the phone call from a friend whose son is at the point of death, a list for shopping that needs to be done first thing tomorrow morning. My mind flits from one to another. Oh, no, they're not *all* bad thoughts. It's just that there are so *many* of them.

What can I do to prevent sensory overload?

First of all, while I believe we need to keep up with what's going on in the world, watching hour after hour of TV news only floods my mind with things I usually can do nothing about. So I must set limits.

Secondly, when friends have big problems in their lives, the best thing I can do for them is to listen intently—and pray. Even there, I've learned I need to set time limits.

Keeping paper and pencil beside the bed for jotting down in the night those things you just remembered that you need to do can better put them out of your mind until morning. Writing them down will probably let you go back to sleep.

Ultimately, however, if you're going to find peace, you have to replace bothersome thoughts with the eternal truths of God's Word. Truths like, "You keep him in perfect peace whose mind is stayed on you, because he trusts in you" (Isaiah 26:3). Old standbys like "casting all your anxieties on him, because he cares for you" (1 Peter 5:7). The Bible tells us to "take every thought captive to obey Christ" (2 Corinthians 10:5).

Yes, in this day and age we keep in touch with what's going on in our world more than ever before. But there comes a time when you have to bring those thoughts into captivity to Christ. I like the way my mom put it: "God, if *You* never go to sleep, then there's no use both of us staying awake!" So true!

Reflection

Let's let God control our thoughts as well as our actions.

Conversation with God

Lord, I'm so glad I can throw all my anxieties on You because You care for me.

Friendships

By Luisa Reyes-Ampil

There is a friend who sticks closer than a brother.
PROVERBS 18:24

Arlene and Cookie first met each other when they worked together for Cathay Pacific Airways as flight attendants in the mid-1980s. They were merely acquaintances, flying the same routes occasionally and hanging out with other crew members.

Arlene resigned from the airline in the nineties after deciding to take care of her four-month-old baby girl full-time. She flew back to the US, where she and her husband were residing. She and Cookie somehow stayed in touch through common friends who shared news about each of them.

Years later, Arlene suddenly found herself reconnected to Cookie, who moved to the US herself. She, too, had resigned from Cathay Pacific and was now working in financial investments. Cookie extended an invitation to Arlene to join her and her family at church. And for five years, Cookie prayed and never tired of inviting Arlene. . .until that special day finally came.

Arlene and Cookie's friendship now took off. They became kindred spirits because of their faith in Christ and common backgrounds, worshipping in the same church and ministries. God allowed them to go through and share many seasons of life together. Cookie said this of Arlene, "There is nothing like being able to talk about [life] without scathing judgment."

In the Bible, there was a special friendship that existed between David and Jonathan, King Saul's son. "The soul of Jonathan was knit to the soul of David, and Jonathan loved him as his own soul" (1 Samuel 18:1). Eventually, King Saul's jealousy of David's battle victories burned in his heart, leading him to plot against David, and Jonathan angered his father for choosing David's side. Jonathan then warned David, while in hiding. They bitterly wept with each other for the coming separation. "Go in peace, because we have sworn both of us in the name of the LORD, saying, 'The LORD shall be between me and you, and between my offspring and your offspring forever,'" Jonathan said to David before parting ways (1 Samuel 20:42).

David was a loyal friend, and God called him a "man after [His] own heart"! (Acts 13:22 NIV). Yes, God understands our need for friendship—Abraham in the Old Testament was called a "friend of God" (James 2:23). God values friendships, and He knows that we need them!

Reflection

Do you need a true friend? Are you praying for God to send you one?

Conversation with God

Dear Lord, thank You for the friends You blessed me with to share my life!

You've Got Enemies
By Bonnie Sala

Through You we will push down our enemies; through Your name we will trample those who rise up against us. For I will not trust in my bow, nor shall my sword save me. But You have saved us from our enemies, and have put to shame those who hated us. In God we boast all day long, and praise Your name forever.
PSALM 44:5–8 NKJV

I grew up in a peaceful home. Fighting was a rare occurrence, usually involving an argument about doing dishes. When it did occur, the fight invariably ended in a sibling and me having to look each other in the eyes and recite Ephesians 4:32 to each other! ("Be kind to one another, tenderhearted, forgiving one another.") But we do have some fighting to do in this life because, as believers in Christ, we've got enemies. You've got enemies.

Your first enemy is your flesh! Your very own fleshly sin nature seeks to dominate you and produce in you everything but the fruit of the Spirit. "So I say, walk by the Spirit, and you will not gratify the desires of the flesh," we're instructed in Galatians 5:16 (NIV). This requires a daily decision to die to fleshly desires.

And then, there's Satan, who is out to sabotage your thinking. Paul wrote, "But I am afraid that as the serpent deceived Eve by his cunning, your thoughts will be led astray from a sincere and pure devotion to Christ" (2 Corinthians 11:3). Renewing one's mind daily with the Word is nonnegotiable.

Finally, the world seeks to distract you. Its distractions are constant, instantly available, and more glitteringly enticing than ever before—they're as close as the cell phone in your pocket. "Do not love this world nor the things it offers you," we're warned (1 John 2:15 NLT). Purposeful habits, perhaps such as reading your Bible before checking your e-mail, will have to be your strategy here.

Reflection

Which front line of the battle is hardest for you right now?

Conversation with God

Lord, please keep me alert to the battle today, and thank You that through You I can win against my enemies!

Our Generous God
By Luisa Reyes-Ampil

" 'I want to give the one who was hired last the same as I gave
you. Don't I have the right to do what I want with my own
money? Or are you envious because I am generous?' "
MATTHEW 20:14–15 NIV

The owner of a vineyard made five trips to the marketplace to
hire workers, giving us a picture of the size of his property. At the
end of the day, all of the workers received their pay—a denarius
for each one, beginning with those last to be hired and ending
with those that were hired first thing that morning.

What was the reaction of the first hires when they received
their pay? They were upset! "Unfair!" they cried.

The owner of the vineyard responded: "I want to give the
one who was hired last the same as I gave you. Don't I have the
right to do what I want with my own money? Or are you envious
because I am generous?" (Matthew 20:14–15 NIV). Consider what
the landowner is really saying.

"I want to give the same" means *I choose to give to all equally.*

"I have the right to do what I want" says *I have the authority
to do what I choose. I am the decision maker, not you.*

And, "Are you envious because I am generous?" simply put
is *Who are you to challenge my decision when I have given you
more than you deserve?*

Our heavenly Father calls us to Himself so that we can be

with Him in heaven—for eternity. We were shown the same mercy when we received His offer of salvation through Jesus Christ, but we didn't all respond at the same time. Some said yes right away; others responded just now. Still others will take His offer on their deathbeds. But no matter when the offer is accepted, the destination will not change. Heaven will be there as promised! It is big enough to house as many as come to Him. God offers the same love and gift of grace.

Reflection ────────────

If you have been in relationship with Christ for most of your life, how can you watch for wrong responses in yourself to people who you think do not deserve salvation?

Conversation with God ────────

Lord, thank You for the reminder of how generous You are to forgive me and to offer me eternal life through Jesus Christ. Help me to have Your heart for people and not to criticize those who are slow to accept You.

Chained with Words

By Bonnie Sala

The tongue can bring death or life;
those who love to talk will reap the consequences.
PROVERBS 18:21 NLT

It was a shocking story that gripped the nation. In 2002, fourteen-year-old Elizabeth Smart was abducted at knifepoint from her bed in the middle of the night in Salt Lake City, Utah. Her family searched for her in vain. Nine months later she was eventually recognized on a street with her abductor.

For some time, Smart was kept chained to a tree. But eventually chains were unnecessary to keep her from fleeing. Words were enough. Her captor constantly threatened to kill her family if she did not comply with his demands. "I have been chained up with actual chains but I have also been chained with words and I can tell you that words are so much stronger than actual chains,"[95] she later recounted.

The Bible speaks very realistically about the power of the tongue. "And among all the parts of the body, the tongue is a flame of fire. It is a whole world of wickedness, corrupting your entire body. It can set your whole life on fire, for it is set on fire by hell itself. . . But no one can tame the tongue. It is restless

95 "Elizabeth Smart Says Kidnapper Was a 'Master at Manipulation,'" NPR, October 8, 2013, accessed November 23, 2016, http://www.npr.org/2013/10/08/230204193/elizabeth-smart-says-kidnapper-was-a-master-at-manipulation.

and evil, full of deadly poison" (James 3:6, 8 NLT).

And yet, words can be life-giving blessings: "Gracious words are like a honeycomb, sweetness to the soul and health to the body" (Proverbs 16:24). Proverbs 25:11 paints my favorite word picture: "A word fitly spoken is like apples of gold in a setting of silver." Watching my own words is a struggle; I can be bitingly sarcastic and forget to encourage others verbally. Once, to reach my kids with an object lesson (ahem, no. . .really for my own reminder), I painted an apple with gold paint, set it in a silver bowl, and placed it on the kitchen counter. "Set a guard, O LORD, over my mouth; keep watch over the door of my lips" is my personal verse (Psalm 141:3)!

But what are the characteristics of wholesome words?

1. They build people up (Ephesians 4:29).
2. They are grace giving (Colossians 4:6).
3. They are spoken at the right time (Proverbs 15:23).

Reflection

Do your words hurt or help those closest to you?

Conversation with God

Lord, please set a guard over my mouth. Help me to pause and choose words that build others up, seasoned with grace and spoken at the right time!

Use It for My Glory!

By Luisa Reyes-Ampil

> " 'For whoever has will be given more, and they will
> have an abundance. Whoever does not have,
> even what they have will be taken from them.' "
>
> MATTHEW 25:29 NIV

What kind of investments have you made? An educational plan for your children's college? A pension plan for your retirement? Or life insurance for your loved ones should anything happen to you?

Just like all these financial investment plans, we received spiritual gifts, " 'each according to his ability,' " when we said yes to Jesus' offer of salvation (Matthew 25:15 NIV). These spiritual gifts are not burdens of responsibility nor do they lose value over time. They are investments made by God in us for our use in His kingdom on earth. We are called to invest in others in return! But somehow we have a hard time either obeying Him or finding the time to act on investment opportunities. Or we may simply just not know how and what to do.

Here are some investment ideas for using our spiritual gifts:

1. Share the Good News! " 'Go therefore and make disciples of all nations' " (Matthew 28:19).
2. Show God's love for you! " 'You shall love your neighbor as yourself' " (Galatians 5:14).

3. Share your blessings! " 'Truly, I say to you, as you did it to one of the least of these my brothers, you did it to me' " (Matthew 25:40).
4. Take time to touch others! "Religion that is pure and undefiled before God, the Father, is this: to visit orphans and widows in their affliction" (James 1:27).

There are many kinds of investments and different ways of managing them. Our service for the Lord comes in various forms in whatever season of life we are in. You may be a teenager who can play music. You may be a young adult who can help with Sunday school. Or you're a great cook and can be on the hospitality team. You can usher. You can join mission trips. You can be anything in accordance to God's will and call!

Don't be like the servant who hid his one talent that eventually got taken away from him. Remain faithful to your task and to your Master by doing a great job. He gave the talents, and He is definitely watching the increase!

Reflection

What spiritual gifts do you have that you know you can use for God's work?

Conversation with God

I receive Your gifts with pleasure and thanksgiving, Lord. Help me to grow where You plant me so I can do the work You want me to do.

Shameless

By Luisa Reyes-Ampil

And the man and his wife hid themselves from the presence
of the LORD God among the trees of the garden.
GENESIS 3:8

Showtime's series called *Shameless* is just that—shameless! The series revolves around an alcoholic single dad in a perpetual drunken state while his six children survive on their own resourcefulness living in a horrible environment. The family is so dysfunctional that a smart daughter did term papers and took tests for others for easy money. One son traded tutorial services for free sex with the neighborhood girls. And another son is a sociopath and loves to play with fire. The rest of the Gallagher kids lived out their own issues as well. This successful series plays right into today's reality.

Sadly, we're often surrounded by shameless behavior in this world: a teenage skateboarder intentionally crosses your car's path while lighting his joint; a single mom outrageously flirts with her daughter's cheerleading coach in front of everyone; two people making out block the sidewalk; airline passengers disregard the flight attendant's instructions and have to be told repeatedly to take their seats and fasten their seatbelts because the plane is still taxiing to the arrival gate.

Shamelessness happened for the first time when two people decided to eat from the tree of the knowledge of good and evil after a very strict directive from God not to. When Adam and Eve ate of the forbidden fruit, their eyes "were opened, and they knew that they were naked. And they sewed fig leaves together and made themselves loincloths" (Genesis 3:7).

Let's remember that "the wrath of God is revealed from heaven against all ungodliness and unrighteousness of men, who by their unrighteousness suppress the truth" (Romans 1:18). This behavior comes from people who do not acknowledge God, so He "gave them up to a debased mind to do what ought not to be done" (v. 28). But as believers in Christ we should strive to live righteously by faith and continue to uphold the truth that lives in us.

Reflection

On your journey into grace, is there any shameless activity that you need to give up today?

Conversation with God

Hide me, O Lord, in Your Word so that I will not be ashamed of my actions. Help me to honor You.

Why I Reread My Own Books
By Darlene Sala

*"For it is precept upon precept, precept upon precept,
line upon line, line upon line, here a little, there a little."*
ISAIAH 28:10

I love meeting in person the people who've read the books I write. Sometimes they'll even say they've read a book several times. I thank them for sharing because it's an encouragement for me to learn that my written words have blessed someone else.

Sometimes I'll add, "You know, I read the books again, too, because I haven't learned all those lessons yet." I'm usually answered by a half smile and an incredulous look that communicates they don't believe me that I reread my own books. But it's true. You see, most of what I write comes from reading God's Word in my personal quiet time with the Lord. The best way I can describe those times is that God seems to open a window on a verse in the Bible so that His light shines in, and I begin to understand better what He is saying.

Then I think, *Maybe someone else could be helped by those thoughts, too,* and I jot down the ideas for a devotional selection for a new book. But does that mean I've learned the lesson God is teaching me so that I never have to apply that scripture again? Oh no—not in any way. I'm a slow learner. I have to read something again and again for the truth to become part of my life.

Like you, I'm on a journey toward understanding the life

God wants me to live. And I certainly haven't arrived yet. I like to call it "a journey into grace."

That's why as you read your Bible, it's a good idea also to journal. If you do, you won't waste any of the truth God is teaching you through His Word. You can go back and reread those lessons over and over again.

We're all seeking answers. So, take each truth God shows you, write it down, and put it into practice. And, yes, it's okay—in fact, it's a good idea—to go back a few months later and reread what you've written.

Reflection _____

What is the latest truth God showed you from His Word?

Conversation with God _____

Thank You for the Bible—so full of guidance and encouragement! Show me what truth You want me to apply to my life today, and then help me to be obedient.

Gotcha!

By Luisa Reyes-Ampil

"You shall have no other gods before me.
You shall not make for yourself a carved image."
EXODUS 20:3-4

We humans are funny. We like to be prepared. Just think of the Bring-Me game that is often played at baby and wedding showers. Don't you like to come prepared, so you stuff your purse with an old photo of yourself, a safety pin, and a foreign coin, *just in case*?

In our old home in Makati, Philippines, we had statues of saints in almost all the rooms. Some of them were made of ivory; some were antiques. One image was used for praying for lost things. Another was used for praying for a good voyage. And still another just for a special petition. We even participated in home visitations of the Virgin Mary statue for a week! Yes, we wanted to cover every aspect of life!

Paul saw how religious the Athenians were by the graven images all over. But Paul came even better prepared, having been equipped by the Holy Spirit for the tough work ahead of him wherever he was sent. He came with a sharp eye and mind. "For as I passed along and observed the objects of your worship, I found also an altar with this inscription: 'To the unknown god' " (Acts 17:23). The Athenians were trying to cover their bases and didn't want to offend a god that they might miss; hence, they included a random image to worship. And Paul seized this very opportunity by claiming the "unknown" god to be the one and only true God! So he presented the Gospel as well as taught them the worship of God in spirit and in truth.

Gotcha! Paul's presentation of the Gospel to the Athenians opened their eyes to the true way to worship God. God's commandment states clearly that we are not to make any graven image, more so not to bow to and serve one. We *are* the living saints as believers in Jesus Christ, not the graven images made by hand found in many homes and churches.

We need to submit to God's holy commandment, remembering that He is the one true God who deserves our full attention and worship. He alone is worthy of our praise!

Reflection

Are you relying on anything other than God for your needs?

Conversation with God

Lord, thank You that You are all I need for every issue that will ever arise in my life! Thank You that You are a prayer away.

Make an Acceptable Offering
By Luisa Reyes-Ampil

Let the words of my mouth and the meditation of my heart be acceptable in your sight, O LORD, my rock and my redeemer.
PSALM 19:14

I once heard a curious question as I listened to a call-in radio show called the *Pastors' Perspective*. The caller, a church leader, wanted advice from the pastors hosting the show regarding a member of his church. The question concerned a woman who was known to be a fortune-teller yet who gave her tithe regularly. Instead of putting the tithe in the offering, she would personally hand it to the leaders, making sure that they knew how she earned it. The question was *Should they turn down this gift knowing where it came from?*

When Paul arrived in Ephesus, he shared the Gospel of Jesus Christ for two years. However, there were still believers who continued in their wickedness until "fear fell upon them all, and the name of the Lord Jesus was extolled. Also many of those who were now believers came, confessing and divulging their practices. And a number of those who had practiced magic arts brought their books together and burned them in the sight of all" (Acts 19:17–19).

How in the world can a Christian be endowed with the Holy Spirit when he is still joined at the hip to the powers of this world? Have you ever heard people joke about the Mafia giving donations to the church so that their sins can be forgiven and the blood on their hands washed clean? The fortune-teller may "cheerfully" give her offering, but the very source of the money seems to be an affront to the one true God. Until we lovingly confront perverse reasoning with God's Word, it will be difficult for this "believer" to understand and embrace God's teachings completely.

"Well, I certainly wouldn't have anything to do with *witchcraft*," you may say. But would we want to review our TV program lineup with our pastor? Or invite the church elder board over for a party with our friends from work?

Reflection

Are you able to bring the whole of your life to God as an "acceptable offering"?

Conversation with God

Dear Father, how foolish we are to pass on "unclean" things to You, including our own selves. Help us to set things right with You so that we bring ourselves to You as an acceptable offering.

Prayer, Praise, and Presence

The practices that won't change your circumstances, but they'll change you

Mornings

By Bonnie Sala

---

*Let me hear of your unfailing love each morning, for I am
trusting you. Show me where to walk, for I give myself to you.*
PSALM 143:8 NLT

My mom always used to say that she had a least favorite time
of the day: four o'clock in the afternoon. The day was waning
but not quite over, everyone was tired and hungry, and by that
time she realized she wasn't going to get everything done she
thought she would have!

I, on the other hand, have a truly *favorite* time of day: seven
thirty in the morning. At this time of the day, the air is fresh, the
sun is gently warming up the earth, birds are singing, and
the day lies before me as one giant possibility. Mornings get
some prominent billing in God's Word: His mercies are new
every morning (Lamentations 3:23). Joy comes in the morning
(Psalm 30:5). The Word of the Lord often comes in the morning
(Ezekiel 12:8).

In fact, there are a disturbingly large number of verses
talking about people rising *"very early* in the morning"! Like
Jesus, for example. Mark 1:35 tells us that "very early in the
morning, while it was still dark, Jesus got up, left the house and
went off to a solitary place, where he prayed" (Mark 1:35 NIV).
And "all the people came early in the morning to hear him at
the temple" (Luke 21:38 NIV).

In the quiet of the morning, I have an opportunity, not necessarily to set the course of my day, but to allow the Holy Spirit to change the "me" that goes through the day. But it's more than a nice idea; this habit has two benefits:

1. When I begin my day by focusing on His unfailing love for me, His trustworthiness and the assurance of His direction as I go forth, I'm reminded that my responses to the day don't have to come from my own limited strength. (Doing my days solely in my flesh never ends well.) I need to say, "I am trusting You. Show me where to walk, for I give myself to You."
2. I begin my day satisfied. I have done the most important thing, the *only truly needed thing.*

Reflection

Do you notice the difference in your day, your life, when your morning begins with Jesus and His Word?

Conversation with God

Lord, help me to develop the discipline and the yearning to wake up to You! I thank You for Your unfailing love for me. I trust You, and I look to You today to guide me just where I need to go and to do just what You have for me to do.

Made for Relationship
By Bonnie Sala

*He makes the whole body fit together perfectly. As each
part does its own special work, it helps the other parts grow,
so that the whole body is healthy and growing and full of love.*
EPHESIANS 4:16 NLT

As crazy as it sounds, God made us because He wanted to have
relationship with us—He wanted to love us. He made us *for
relationship, for love*, which is why we feel so terrible when we
are lacking in either. He made us to need Him and to need one
another. That's why he called His people the body of Christ:
eyes, ears, legs, and lips, we are all different and designed to
rely on each other.

But even though we are members of that body, sometimes
we can feel disconnected. We can be lonely, very lonely, at
church. And the enemy of our faith, our enemy, likes it that way!
Author Anita Lustrea says it's because "we are in a battle, and
Satan desperately wants to keep us from building relationships
that will fortify our faith and strengthen us spiritually. If he can
keep community from being built he will have succeeded. . .
[for] his plan is to isolate us and take us out of commission."[96]

As long as we are isolated, doing life all on our own, we miss
the growth, health, and love God intended for us to receive. But
even more, we need to do daily life with other believers in order

96 Lustrea, *What Women Tell Me*, 25.

to be able to truly see ourselves. Lustrea notes, "C. S. Lewis said it best, '…He works on us through each other. Men are mirrors, or carriers of Christ to other men. Sometimes unconscious carriers.' When we are in community, we are mirrors for each other. When we walk the path alone, we don't have true perspective, because God made us for community."[97]

We see ourselves and we come to see different aspects of Jesus' character in the lives of others who *aren't* like us. In the lives of other believers, I come to understand the scope and variety of the different ways God works: the ways He speaks, the ways He meets needs, and the ways He leads.

Reflection

Have you seen Jesus in a sister you journey with?

Conversation with God

Father, help me to reach out to others with my needs and to meet theirs. If I need community, please send me friends in You to journey with.

---

97 Ibid., 36.

The Giver, Not the Gift

By Luisa Reyes-Ampil

And Jabez called on the God of Israel saying, "Oh, that You would bless me indeed, and enlarge my territory, that Your hand would be with me, and that You would keep me from evil, that I may not cause pain!" So God granted him what he requested.

1 CHRONICLES 4:10 NKJV

Bruce Wilkinson wrote a mini book called *The Prayer of Jabez* several years ago. Many started claiming the prayer for themselves—posting the prayer all over their homes, cars, and workplaces—until *The Cult of Jabez* by Steve Hopkins was released. Although I have not personally read either book, I can fairly judge the contents from the titles.

Is it not right for us to claim blessings? That all depends on why you are asking for them! The problem is the focus on material prosperity. Jabez was most likely asking the Lord to show him more ways he could serve and honor Him instead of material wealth for himself since he "was more honorable than his brothers" (1 Chronicles 4:9). And God honored and blessed him. But many have taken that verse out of context.

The refrain of the song "The Prayer of Jabez" by musical group According to John goes, "Father bless me indeed! You're all that I need. Expand my horizon beyond what I can see. Put Your hand upon me and keep me from evil. This is what I pray."[98]

98 John Mihaiu, "Song of Jabez," Christian Lyrics Online, 2010, accessed December 15, 2016, http://www.christianlyricsonline.com/artists/according-to-john/song-of-jabez.html.

Those lyrics tell me to pray for the following: (1) surrender and dependence on the Lord because He is all I need in life; (2) wisdom to see beyond my circumstances because God has something better in store for me that I may not see now—my eternal inheritance; and (3) guidance in my daily walk as I cannot do righteous things on my own.

"It is important to remember that the Giver, the Lord, is more important than the gift. If we focus solely on the request of Jabez, it could be easy to make the mistake of turning it into a formula for obtaining what we want from God."[99] There you have it! Blessing is not just about financial wealth!

Reflection

What is it that you are asking the Lord to give you today?

Conversation with God

Lord, I know that it is better for me to ask for Your will to be done in my life instead of asking merely for material wealth. I ask that You make it clearly known to me that this is best for me so that I do not ask for what is not important.

---

99 Albert Lee, "Who Is Jabez?" *Our Daily Bread*, January 29, 2003, accessed December 15, 2016, http://odb.org/2003/01/29/who-is-jabez/.

Alone

By Bonnie Sala

But when he was alone with his own disciples,
he explained everything.
MARK 4:34 NIV

Depending on the circumstances and your temperament, being alone can be a calm, peaceful state or a destitute, painful place to be. Yet it's when we are by ourselves that we seem to be able to do our best thinking. Jesus modeled this alone time for us, jumping into a boat to leave the crowds across the Sea of Galilee or heading up into the garden of Gethsemane to be with His Father in prayer.

We read: "But Jesus often withdrew to lonely places and prayed" (Luke 5:16 NIV), and "Jesus got up, left the house and went off to a solitary place, where he prayed" (Mark 1:35 NIV). Now, it can be hard to find somewhere to be alone—it was for Jesus. You might remember the old King James Version of Matthew 6:6: "But thou, when thou prayest, enter into thy closet, and when thou hast shut thy door, pray to thy Father which is in secret." For several years, my "prayer closet" was actually a real clothes closet where I could sit and close the door behind me!

When we are "too busy" to commune alone with Him, "God will keep harrowing us in until He gets us alone. . . . He will take us through the disappointment of a wounded pride of intellect, through disappointment of heart. He will reveal inordinate affections—things over which we never thought He would have to, to get us alone,"[100] explains the great Christian writer Oswald Chambers.

It's because of love. When two people are in love, they want to be alone together, to concentrate only on each other. So God's love for you and His plan for you are intensely personal. Spend time alone with Him today. "Our fellowship with God is not meant to wait until we are in heaven."[101]

Reflection

What, if anything, is stopping you from spending daily time alone with God and His Word? Where can you go to hear His voice?

Conversation with God

Lord, I do want to be alone with You. Help me to order my life in a way that allows time for me to hear Your voice.

100 Oswald Chambers, "Have You Ever Been Alone with God?" *My Utmost for His Highest*, January 12, 2016, accessed November 26, 2016, http://utmost.org/classic/have-you-ever-been-alone-with-god-classic.

101 John MacArthur Jr, quoted in "Alone with God," Goodreads, accessed December 4, 2016, https://www.goodreads.com/work/quotes/427048-alone-with-god-macarthur-study-series.

Study the Promises

By Darlene Sala

He has granted to us his precious and very great promises.
2 PETER 1:4

Ruth Graham, beloved wife of evangelist Billy Graham, tells of being jolted awake suddenly in the night by the name of someone she loved dearly who was trying hard to run away from God. In the darkness her fears ran rampant.

"Suddenly the Lord said to me, 'Quit studying the problems and start studying the promises.' "

Can you identify with her reaction? Yes, sometimes we spend more time worrying about the problem than we spend focusing on God's promises to help us with the problem.

The first scripture that came to Ruth's mind was Philippians 4:6–7: "Do not be anxious about anything, but in everything by prayer and supplication with thanksgiving let your requests be made known to God. And the peace of God, which surpasses all understanding, will guard your hearts and your minds in Christ Jesus."

She realized the part she had been neglecting was the phrase "with thanksgiving." Beginning to worship God for who He is and what He is, she found her fears scuttled away like cockroaches when the light is turned on. Peace filled her heart.[102]

102 Ruth Graham, *Letters from Ruth's Attic*, compiled from *Decision Magazine* (Charlotte, NC, 2007), 59.

What are some of those promises? The book of Psalms is full of them. Here are just a few: "Oh, taste and see that the LORD is good! Blessed is the man who takes refuge in him" (Psalm 34:8). "When he calls to me, I will answer him," says God; "I will be with him in trouble; I will rescue him and honor him" (Psalm 91:15). "Those who know your name put their trust in you, for you, O LORD, have not forsaken those who seek you" (Psalm 9:10).

How about Jesus' words in the New Testament? "I tell you, ask, and it will be given to you; seek, and you will find; knock, and it will be opened to you. For everyone who asks receives, and the one who seeks finds, and to the one who knocks it will be opened" (Luke 11:9–10).

When we're troubled about a situation, we're very good at studying the problem. Let's start giving equal time to studying God's promises. You may want to begin listing Bible promises in a notebook or a file on your cellphone or computer. Oh, and don't forget the "with thanksgiving" part. You will find you are encouraged—and you will probably sleep better at night, too.

Reflection

"God never made a promise that was too good to be true." —D. L. Moody[103]

Conversation with God

Help me, Lord, to focus on Your promises, knowing that nothing is too hard for You.

103 Dwight L. Moody, quoted in "Dwight L. Moody Quotes," Brainy Quote, accessed December 1, 2016, https://www.brainyquote.com/quotes/quotes/d/dwightlmo157634.html.

The Practice of Praise

By Bonnie Sala

Great is the LORD, and greatly to be praised;
and his greatness is unsearchable.

PSALM 145:3 KJV

Praise and worship. It's what happens at church before the announcements and the sermon, right? It's that, and *so much more*. We're commanded to praise God about 250 times in the Bible, but not because God is conceited and loves the limelight. The practice of praise puts us in the right position relative to God. It's how we accomplish our chief purpose for being alive: "To glorify God and enjoy Him forever!"[104]

Praising God may be one of the least understood spiritual disciplines of our day. "In genuine spiritual worship we bow before the Most High God, the most merciful and reliable and winsome of all beings, and we crown Him as Lord of all that we are. We consent to His gracious, transforming work in our lives; we agree that He can work in us, so that we'll be willing and able to do His will. In other words, we choose to let Him be God in our lives. This is our greatest privilege, the highest thing we can do."[105]

---

104 The Westminster Assembly, "The Westminster Shorter Catechism," ESVBible.org, accessed December 11, 2016, http://www.esvbible.org/resources/creeds-and-catechisms/article-the-westminster-shorter-catechism/.
105 Ruth Myers and Warren Myers, *31 Days of Praise* (Colorado Springs: Multnomah, 1994), 23.

Praise, worship, thanksgiving: all three overlap as we glorify and enjoy God whether through speaking, singing, or silence. The practice of praise can be cultivated entirely outside the circumstances of our lives because we're told to praise not just for what God *gives* but because of who He is and what He does. "The Bible doesn't command us to feel thankful for every situation. It doesn't command us to manufacture positive feelings. Instead it commands us to give thanks (1 Thessalonians 5:18)."[106]

David was a prime *praiser.* He praised God first, then poured out his honest feelings, his complaints, his petitions, concluding again with praise—notice the pattern in Psalm 42. He chose to keep on praising in spite of how things seemed. If you will cultivate this habit it will change you!

"Before you go out into the world, wash your face in the clear crystal water of praise. Bury each yesterday in the fine linen and spices of thankfulness."[107] Yes, you can pause to praise Him as you rise in the morning, whisper it throughout the day, and breathe it as your last thought of the night.

Reflection

Will you try the *praise challenge* for one month?

Conversation with God

Lord, I want You to be fully God in my life. Teach me the practice of praise!

---

106 Ibid., 26.
107 Charles Spurgeon, quoted in "Praise and Thankfulness," *Elisabeth Elliot Newsletter* (July/August 2002), accessed December 11, 2016, http://www.elisabethelliot.org/newsletters/2002-07-08.pdf.

Intentional Prayer Time

By Luisa Reyes-Ampil

After he had dismissed the crowds, he went
up on the mountain by himself to pray.
MATTHEW 14:23

Can you imagine being asked to leave? And that is exactly what Jesus did to the crowd of five thousand that came to gather to see and hear Him! *What's up with Jesus? Was He tired and just having a bad day?*

Before this incident happened, Jesus received news of John the Baptist's beheading and "he withdrew by boat privately to a solitary place" (v. 13 NIV). But the crowds followed Him, and when He saw them, "he had compassion on them and healed their sick" (v. 14 NIV). However, Jesus knew His priorities. He needed time to be by Himself and be with His Father. He needed to pray! And the only way He could do that was to say, "Look, you need to leave now."

Very often we are embarrassed to tell the truth when we are tired or sick or busy. We do not want to offend people, so we just pretend everything's okay. We also want to think that we are doing the right thing by being selfless. So we set aside our plans and get behind schedule. We only have ourselves to blame for not being able to accomplish what we intended and needed to do.

This story reminded me again that the reason I have

difficulties sticking to my quiet time is because I don't make time for it. Prayer time should be intentional. I have to make a conscious effort to pray, so I need to block off that holy hour. I find this to be a constant struggle. When it's time to be alone with Jesus and pray, I'll see something out of place at home and start cleaning up. By the time I am done, I have eaten up my quiet time and have to watch the clock very closely in order to be on time for work.

Jesus knew when to say no, and we must learn to do the same thing. After all, prayer is very important because without it we cannot communicate with our Father, hear what He has to say about our day, and find the assurance that today is really His.

Reflection

What one thing keeps you away from your quiet time?

Conversation with God

Thank You, Jesus, for teaching us to set aside time to talk to You and lay everything at Your feet. Help me to learn how to give You my worries, anxieties, and stressful instances so I can focus and make You my priority. And, most importantly, to never be too busy to have time with You.

He Prayed Again

By Bonnie Sala

And again he went away and prayed,
saying the same words.

MARK 14:39

When we think of the example Jesus set for us in prayer, we naturally think of the pattern set down for us in the Lord's Prayer. But the Gospel of Mark contains a powerful example of another principle of prayer that Jesus demonstrated for us when He was at His very worst, His very lowest and most dread-filled hour spent as God and man on earth.

It happened right after dinner, after the Last Supper. It seems hard to imagine that Jesus enjoyed that meal very much, but perhaps He did, as it was the last good amount of time He would spend with those He loved. The party headed to the garden of Gethsemane, which still exists today on a hillside in Jerusalem. Leaving the majority under the olive trees, He took the inner circle of Peter, James, and John a little farther into the garden, telling them, "My soul is crushed with grief to the point of death. Stay here and keep watch with me (Mark 14:34 NLT).

Jesus, the Son of God, was completely overcome, flooded with pain at what He knew was approaching, so much so that after He walked a bit farther, He couldn't even stand up—He fell to the ground. "Abba, Father!" He cried out. "Is there ANY way You can do this without the cross? Every fiber of My humanity cries 'NO!' " (paraphrase mine). "Yet, I want Your will to be done, not mine."

This alone would have been such a powerful example for me—knowing that Jesus understands the pain I have faced in my life, the struggle between my flesh and what I know is God's best for me. He understands when I inwardly scream, "No! Just no," to things God has allowed on my journey. But the truth that was really surprising to me is in Mark 14:39. After Jesus returned and found the faithful sleeping, He *went away and prayed, saying the same words* (emphasis added).

As Jesus continued to ask the Father for the same thing over and over again, so I, too, can continue in my petitions! This was not the rote repetition of some memorized prayer but the ongoing cry of His heart that long night. The Father did not tire of Jesus' prayer, and He does not tire of mine either!

Reflection

Is there an issue in your life that you have been reluctant to keep praying about?

Conversation with God

Jesus, thank You for Your willingness to be God and man, to teach us there is never a limit to petitioning our Father!

Don't Take It Back!

By Luisa Reyes-Ampil

But if we hope for what we do not
yet have, we wait for it patiently.
ROMANS 8:25 NIV

I was talking on the phone with my prayer partner, Dee, on my way to work one morning, checking up on God's answers to our prayer items. She asked about one that has been on my list for almost a year.

"How's the job search for so-and-so?"

"Nothing yet! Still searching and waiting. I am getting tired, Dee. Tonight I will ask so-and-so about goals and make sure there is a deadline for accomplishing them. I have overextended my home, and my hospitality has run out!" I was getting more upset by the minute.

"Aren't we praying about this?" Dee countered.

"Yes, but. . ." I stumbled.

"Well, Luisa," Dee said, "go ahead and take it back from God. Let me know what happens after your talk." And we said our good-byes.

When I got home, I was ready for my confrontation until I was met with this: "I have a temp job that starts tomorrow. The hours are 12 midnight to 8:00 a.m."

Hallelujah! The Lord just shut me up after I plotted to take the problem back into my own hands, to come up with my own solution to the problem that I had been asking Him to answer!

How often do we stay on track with our commitment to pray about something? We start off strong and keep on until we tire and run out of ways of asking for the same thing, thinking the Lord is getting tired as well. Are we praying because we want our prayer answered? What if the Lord is teaching us something first before answering our prayer?

Yes, I have been praying for God's provision of a job for that certain person. But I am forgetting that God is also working on this person, shaping a life whose faith is still immature. Now in my prayers, I ask that God will first show Himself mighty and help with my total surrender so that there is no doubt that whatever provision comes will be attributed to God, and not to human abilities.

As for me, God is teaching me to be patient, a trait that I desperately need to develop. I am a natural problem solver who has a need to fix what is not right—or dispose of something I cannot fix. God spared me from causing a baby Christian to stumble by showing Himself still in control!

Reflection

Have you been praying for something for some time now and getting impatient for God's answer?

Conversation with God

Help me to see, Lord, what I have to learn along the way as I wait for Your answer!

Abide in My Love

By Bonnie Sala

"As the Father has loved me, so have I loved you. Abide in my love."

JOHN 15:9

In his national bestseller—*Love and Respect, The Love She Most Desires; The Respect He Desperately Needs*—Dr. Emerson Eggerichs hits on a principle that resonates with both men and women. Dr. Eggerichs contends that a man's greatest need is for respect and a woman's greatest desire is to feel loved. *Not a real revelation, as far as women are concerned*, you may think. Because. . .love and women. It's what we do. It's who we are. (Admit it: How many text messages did you send with heart emojis this week?)

When we don't feel loved, when we aren't loved, that's when the problems start. When we are looking to other people for love—a spouse, a boyfriend, our children, a friend—we can be sorely disappointed. Perhaps because Jesus knew this, He told us to *abide* in *His* love.

If you abide somewhere, that's where you live. It's where you hang out because you thoroughly enjoy it. Here are some of the things I know about His love that we are to bathe ourselves in:

* He has loved me with a never-ending, everlasting love (Jeremiah 31:3).

* He first loved me (1 John 4:19).

* He proved His love for me by giving Himself for me (Galatians 2:20).

* He loved me so much that, in my original messed-up state, He gave me life (Ephesians 2:4–5).
* He will quiet me by His love (Zephaniah 3:17).
* His love is poured into my heart by the Holy Spirit (Romans 5:5).
* He is abounding in love and that love doesn't change (Psalm 86:15).
* Love comes from Him (1 John 4:7).
* His love is the antidote to fear (1 John 4:18).
* His love reaches to the heavens! (Psalm 36:5).

Which aspect of His love do you need to hang on to today? Are you afraid? Has someone who once loved you betrayed you or rejected you? Are you doubting that you are lovable?

It's crystal clear how He feels about you. He loves you. Write your favorite verse about His love for you on a slip of paper to keep with you for frequent reference. Stay right there in that love today.

Reflection

Do you ever have trouble believing He could love you the way His Word says He does?

Conversation with God

Thank You, Father, for Your love that never ends, that is life-giving, that quiets me, that makes me brave. . .that meets every need of my heart!

Like a Love Letter

By Darlene Sala

Let us then with confidence draw near to the throne of grace,
that we may receive mercy and find grace to help in time of need.
HEBREWS 4:16

I've been thinking about the fact that my brain never seems to turn off. I'm *always* thinking. If I try not to think, I'm only thinking that I'm not thinking! I wonder if God designed us this way so we could truly "pray without ceasing" (1 Thessalonians 5:17). Or at least so we could center our thoughts on God throughout the day—not just at the beginning and end. If that is true, I realize a lot of my brain energy goes to nonessentials. God made me with the potential to fellowship with Him at any time. But do I take advantage of that ability? Not as often as I could or should.

What a privilege! To come into God's presence at any time with everything that concerns me and those I love! "Let us then with confidence draw near to the throne of grace, that we may receive mercy and find grace to help in time of need" (Hebrews 4:16).

I'm afraid most of us pray only when we want something. But I don't think that every prayer should be a request to God for something we want. I know that I don't like it if my own adult kids never call me unless they want something. I wonder if God feels that way, too.

Sometimes our prayers should be like a love letter to the Lord. Other times our prayer should be an experience of friendship or companionship with God—just sitting in His presence and enjoying Him. At times we need to keep quiet and ask Him if there's anything He wants to say to us. Other times we should be lifting up our faces, praising and thanking Him.

To me, praying without ceasing means I'm "online" with God all the time. And I have an unlimited data plan with Him. Aren't you glad God's Internet never goes down! And what does He offer us? The scripture says "mercy and grace" whenever we need them. For me that's pretty much all of the time! You, too?

Reflection _____

What's the one thing you want to include in your letter to God today?

Conversation with God _____

Thank You, Lord, that I can come into Your presence anytime—anywhere—for anything. What a privilege! Help me to remember that today.

At Jesus' Feet
By Bonnie Sala

As Jesus was getting into the boat, the man who
had been demon possessed begged to go with him.
MARK 5:18 NLT

It could have been a scene right out of a horror movie. The naked man lived alone in a graveyard. In fact, no one would even get near him. They had tried, but he was so strong that when they chained him up, he snapped the chains, broke the irons, and fled to the hills, crying out and cutting himself with sharp stones. (Yes, cutting. Do you realize that there's nothing new in Satan's playbook of despair? He still drives people to all types of injury and death every chance he gets.)

But the man in our story (or rather the demons inside the man) saw Jesus from afar, and ran and fell at Jesus' knees. No doubt, the crowd made way for this terrifying spectacle. "Come out of this man, you evil spirit," Jesus said (v. 8 NLT). And then the camera would go in for a close-up; there wasn't just *one* evil spirit tormenting the man. Or even two. "What is your name?" Jesus demanded. "My name is Legion, because there are many of us inside this man" was the answer (v. 9 NLT). It seems impossible to imagine, but yes, there were enough demons to enter two thousand pigs grazing nearby. Off went the demons into the pigs, and off a cliff to their deaths went every single one of those pigs (vv. 12–13).

Can you even imagine the naked, scarred-up man lying limp at Jesus' feet? Where would he begin to piece any kind of a life back together? That's what everyone in the town and countryside wanted to know. They found him, clothed and in his right mind, sitting at Jesus' feet. There was only one place that man wanted to be: at Jesus' feet. When it came time for Jesus to leave, the man *begged* to go with Him!

Reflection

If you have been freed from the sentence of death on your life, you, too, have reason to want to be with Jesus. Has He met needs in your life? Sustained you through sorrow? Given you grace when all of your strength was gone? Does gratitude make you long to be in Jesus' presence?

Conversation with God

God, I am grateful to You for the work that You have done in my life. I surrender to all the freeing work You still desire to do in me, and I rest at Your feet today.

Are You a Cheerleader?

By Luisa Reyes-Ampil

And the women sang to one another as they celebrated, "Saul has struck down his thousands, and David his ten thousands."

1 SAMUEL 18:7

The Elanora Heights Public School in Australia announced their new policy on school spirit. "Instead of clapping, the students are free to punch the air, pull excited faces and wriggle about on the spot."[108] In short, make the motions but not the sounds.

My daughter Christiane was a cheerleader in middle school and high school. She and the rest of the squad rallied the school during games and assemblies. They spent many hours each day throughout almost the entire year learning and practicing routines to music to pump up the crowds and show school spirit.

The Bible is full of active and good cheers! First, let's consider how we can get the crowd going as God goes out to the field and we lift our concerns to Him in prayer.

"Let everything that has breath praise the LORD!" (Psalm 150:6).

"My lips will shout for joy, when I sing praises to you" (Psalm 71:23).

Second, how about when a goal is made and we actually see our answered prayer? I can just hear the band striking up the victory song!

" 'Sing praises to the LORD, for he has done gloriously;

---

108 "Silent School Spirit," *World Magazine* (August 20, 2016): 3.

let this be made known in all the earth' " (Isaiah 12:5).
"And when the builders laid the foundation of the
*temple of the L*ORD*, the priests in their vestments came*
forward with trumpets, and the Levites, the sons of
*Asaph, with cymbals, to praise the L*ORD*" (Ezra 3:10).*

And last, we can't keep to our seats any longer so we stomp our feet, get up from our seats, and stand on the bleachers dancing perhaps as a new life is added to the kingdom!

"[The lame man] stood. . .and entered the temple. . .
walking and leaping and praising God" (Acts 3:8).
"Then I heard. . .the voice of a great multitude. . .
crying out, 'Hallelujah! For the Lord our God the
Almighty reigns' " (Revelation 19:6).

I do cheers for the Lord with my hands lifted high in worship. And if an "old" person like me can't keep myself from clapping, singing, and moving in worship, I wonder how long the Elanora Heights Public School kids will last in their silenced school spirit!

Reflection

Are you a loud cheerleader on God's team or part of the silent school spirit?

Conversation with God

Dear Lord, help me to praise You in everything and to sound Your trumpet always for all to hear!

When Grace Rushes In
By Bonnie Sala

Pride leads to disgrace, but with humility comes wisdom.
PROVERBS 11:2 NLT

Sinful. That wasn't really me. I'd prayed to "ask Jesus into my heart" at age five. My Bible memory verse chart had rows and rows of gold stars for all the verses I'd learned before I was in first grade. I won the "Bring Your Friends to Sunday School" contest hands down (except, since I was the pastor's kid, I couldn't really win the contest and my dad just had to buy me a bike on the side). Then, as if being a pastor's kid wasn't enough, I found myself a missionary kid in a foreign country. That definitely had to count for something, right? Sex, drugs, rock and roll? Not me (well, rock and roll when my parents weren't around). Bible studies? Check. Christian college, Christian spouse? Check. Church leadership? Check.

But by the time I was in my thirties, it all just began to wear thin. On the outside, things looked pretty great. But inside, something began to rot. I knew I didn't really love God. I didn't really love Him—because I had *no real appreciation of what He had done for me*! Jesus said of the woman at the well, "I tell you, her sins—and they are many—have been forgiven, so she has shown me much love. But a person who is forgiven little shows only little love" (Luke 7:47 NLT). I thought I loved Him. I pointed to all the things I did for Him and all the things I *didn't* do! But, what *was* that nasty *smell* seeping out from under all my gift-wrapped, churchy "goodness"? It was the stench of pride.

I didn't know it at the time, but in the years to come, God would choose to use humiliating circumstances to bring my life down with a crash, to move me to the place where I realized any good in my life was His work in me. "To be humbled really means to be humiliated," wrote Ron Mehl. "People who are truly humble are often humiliated while trying to perform the task to which they've been called. They're embarrassed to even admit to trying. They realize that God will have to basically underwrite the whole thing or it will never be done. Period."[109]

When pride is removed, grace rushes in.

Reflection

Is there an area of your life where you think you've "got it together"? Ask God to point out any reliance on your own strength today.

Conversation with God

Thank You for loving me enough to show me where I need less of me and more of You.

---

109 Ron Mehl, *Surprise Endings: Ten Good Things about Bad Things* (Colorado Springs: Multnomah, 1995), 75.

Is Prayer Enough?

By Darlene Sala

*On him we have set our hope that he will continue
to deliver us, as you help us by your prayers.*
2 CORINTHIANS 1:10–11 NIV

Allie Pohlmeier Smith served for a period of time as a missionary in Kenya. After she returned to the United States, violence broke out in the country she had grown to love. As the atrocities mounted, her heart ached to help. Yet, all she could do was pray. And pray she did. But she became haunted by that thought, *All we can do is pray.*

Really? Is that all we can do? she thought to herself. *Is it enough? I was thinking more on the lines of jumping on a plane.*

In a newsletter she asks, "How often when you find yourself in the midst of something difficult do you hear 'prayer is powerful' or 'all you can do is pray'? Did that truth offer any comfort or was it merely a cheer from the Christian pom squad?"

Allie opened her Bible for answers and found 2 Corinthians 1:10–11 (NIV): "He has delivered us from such a deadly peril, and he will deliver us again. On him we have set our hope that he will continue to deliver us, *as you help us by your prayers*" (emphasis added).

Later she heard from the pastor of a tin, plastic, and wood church in Kibera that had been in the middle of a huge market in that slum city. The entire market had burned down—Allie saw the pictures on the BBC. Yet the pastor saw what happened as "the Lord taking over." While the building was gone, the real "church"—the congregation—was still standing. Their homes and all their possessions were burned or looted, but no one lost their life, including the small children. "Only God we depend on," said the pastor. "The 'church' is still standing. They tried to burn it with fire, but fire can't burn it."[110]

I admit that I don't know how prayer works, but I know we are commanded in scripture to pray. And that is enough. In obedience to God's instruction, we pray, and our mighty God answers. He has designed this privilege of communication with Himself in such a way that we truly can help others with our prayers. He promises this in His Word!

Are you praying for someone who is desperate for help from God? Don't stop!

Reflection

"Fervent prayers produce phenomenal results." —Woodrow Kroll[111]

Conversation with God

Thank You, Lord, for the privilege of prayer. I'm waiting for Your miracles in the lives of people I love.

---

110 Allie Pohlmeier Smith, "*Is Prayer Enough for Kenya?*" Wrecked for the Ordinary, March 26, 2008, accessed March 14, 2017, www.wrecked.org/culture/Kenya-needs-our-prayers-and-more/.

111 Woodrow Kroll, quoted in "22 Motivating Quotes about Prayer," Christian Quotes, accessed November 13, 2016, http://www.christianquotes.info/top-quotes/22-motivating-quotes-about-prayer/.

The Work of Gratitude
By Bonnie Sala

*Be thankful in all circumstances, for this is
God's will for you who belong to Christ Jesus.*
1 THESSALONIANS 5:18 NLT

Author Ann Voskamp's book *One Thousand Gifts* has had a huge impact. Women (and I suppose some men) went out and bought notebooks in which to daily record all the gifts in their lives that they were thankful for. I kept at it until my list topped a thousand. . .and the exercise had a huge effect on my eyesight—the eyesight of my soul. When you're really on the hunt for God's blessings in your life, you begin to see them everywhere: rain-sweetened air, pineapple, a long hug from my son, a hair appointment, my neighbor's purple vine. After I developed the "eyesight" to see them, the first thing I learned is that God's gifts to me are abundant and continuously given. I like to call them "handfuls of grace."

I also learned that His gifts are present even in the midst of trying circumstances. First Thessalonians 5:18 had always been familiar to me: "Be thankful in all circumstances," but suddenly that little word *in* became very important to me. The hard, the painful times are as much parts of the journey as the joy and the blessings. Although I might have a hard time thanking God *for* all of the circumstances of my journey, I could certainly thank Him *in* the circumstances. Because there are always handfuls of grace in the life of the believer.

"Thanksgiving in all things accepts the deep mystery of God through everything," Voskamp writes in her blog. "We give thanks to God not because of how we feel but because of Who He is. No amount of regret changes the past, no amount of anxiety changes the future, but any amount of gratitude changes the present. In stressful times, seek God. In painful times, praise God. In the terrible times, trust God. And at all times...*thank God*."[112]

Recognizing who God is and watching for His gifts changes me. Gratitude changes me right now, in whatever mess I am in. Giving thanks makes me mindful of His involvement in my life, and noting even the smallest of His gifts reminds me of His great love. I *can* give thanks *in all things*!

Reflection

Have you discovered the power of thanking God in all things?

Conversation with God

God, I do thank You for who You are. I thank You for Your love and the gifts You give daily. Help me to see them, to see Your hand as I respond with gratitude in all that comes to me.

---

112 Ann Voskamp, "Holiday Conversations around the Table Have You Worried? Try This," Annvoskamp.com, November 23, 2016, accessed November 25, 2016, http://annvoskamp.com/2016/11/holiday-conversations-around-the-table-have-you-worried-try-this/.

Home!

By Darlene Sala

"If anyone loves me, he will keep my word, and my Father will love him, and we will come to him and make our home with him."

JOHN 14:23

Did you ever think of God as being at home with you every day? Yet, that's what He offers us. What an amazing thought that the Creator of the universe, who owns *everything*, wants to be at home with *me*!

But He doesn't offer to come just as a visitor on vacation. He wants a permanent residency. I like what Max Lucado wrote:

> *God wants to be your dwelling place. He has no interest in being a weekend getaway or a Sunday bungalow or a summer cottage. Don't consider using God as a vacation cabin or an eventual retirement home. . . . He wants to be the one in whom "we live and move and have our being" (Acts 17:28 NIV).*[113]

That might make you feel a bit uncomfortable—God living with you and you with Him day in and day out. But it's really an amazing privilege. Especially when you realize He knows us inside out—the good, the bad, and everything in between. And

---

113 Max Lucado, *Grace for the Moment* (Nashville: Countryman, a division of Thomas Nelson Inc., 2000), January 6 selection.

yet He still loves us.

Being human as we are, it's easy to think of God being way up in heaven and us being way down here on earth—far from each other. But that's not God's idea of a relationship. Colossians 1:27 has a little phrase that is full of meaning: "Christ in you, the hope of glory"—the closeness of living together every moment of every day.

The only requirement is that we love and obey Him. That isn't asking too much after all He's done for us, is it? He always knows what is best for us anyway. Maybe today is the day you take up His offer and accept a marvelous bond with Him as His child and He as your Father. Or if you already have a relationship with Jesus, maybe you just want to ask Him to do a little housecleaning. You could start by admitting that sometimes He hasn't been first in your life but you want that to change. Jesus assures you that if you love Him and keep His Word, the Father will love you and make His home with you. In fact, it's a promise.

Reflection

Just think about the Lord making His home with you and me. What an honor!

Conversation with God

Dear Lord, right now I invite You to have the supreme place in my life.

Life's Greatest Romance

By Bonnie Sala

"I have loved you with an everlasting love;
I have drawn you with unfailing kindness."

JEREMIAH 31:3 NIV

Rainbow Cottage by Grace Livingston Hill was the first romance novel I ever read as a young girl. It was sweet, if predictable; the would-be groom was rich and the story ended in a perfect marriage, living happily ever after in the Rainbow Cottage. I went on to collect vintage first editions of these Christian romance novels with colorful art deco covers. So, of course I looked for my own prince. But God had a much greater romance waiting for me.

"Get into the habit of saying, 'Speak, Lord,'" wrote Oswald Chambers, "and life will become a romance."[114] This is true. The path to this greater romance, however, wasn't strewn with rose petals. It was often watered with tears. At first I cried, "Speak, oh please speak! Please hear my cry and help me!" And He did hear and He did speak to me in my dire need.

To teach me the habit of going to Him and waiting, God provided day after day and then year after year of circumstances that pressed me to His side. Each day my reading from His *love letter*, His Word, was frequently, intimately applicable to my circumstance, addressing my deepest needs. I began to know

---

114 Oswald Chambers, "My Utmost for His Highest: Devotional for January 30," Studylight. org, accessed December 1, 2016, https://www.studylight.org/devotionals/utm/?d=0130.

His love as I had never known possible. Unlike the love of human princes, His love does not fail; His love alone is everlasting! My heart is truly safe in His hands.

Have you been disappointed by human love? In some ways, entering into this relationship involves giving up expectations of human love, realizing that *no* human love, no romance between two people, will ever meet our deepest needs. To be fair, human relationships weren't designed to do what only God can do in our lives. In fact, relationships between men and women invariably improve when we look to God's love to meet our deepest needs.

We can run to Him and cry out: "Satisfy us each morning with your unfailing love, so we may sing for joy to the end of our lives" (Psalm 90:14 NLT). Maybe you need to continue: "Give us gladness in proportion to our former misery! Replace the evil years with good" (v. 15 NLT).

Yes, speak, Lord, that we may experience life's greatest romance.

Reflection
Have you experienced life's greatest romance?

Conversation with God
O God, thank You that You long to draw us with kindness to Your love—to life's greatest romance—if we will but come to You, read Your love letter, and call on Your name.

In All Respects His Favorite

By Bonnie Sala

And so I walk in the LORD's presence as I live here on earth!
PSALM 116:9 NLT

Shortly after my grandfather graduated to heaven, I found a small, leather-bound book among his things. *Practicing the Presence of God* was embossed in gold on the cover. Written in the sixteenth century by a layman who served in a monastery, it's a small collection of letters, yet they give us some beautiful pictures of our relationship with God. He called himself Brother Lawrence.

Brother Lawrence had had an epiphany while gazing at a tree in the midst of winter. Stripped of its leaves, the tree looked, for all intents and purposes, dead. But he knew that in only a little time life would once again infuse its limbs, green leaves would be renewed, and after that, flowers and fruit. Life had never left the tree just as God's presence redeems the believer's life from death and never leaves us.

Brother Lawrence's work in the monastery was simple: he was a cook and a sandal maker. His intention in entering the monastery was to sacrifice his life and all pleasures to God. God, however, disappointed Lawrence, for he "met with nothing but satisfaction in that state." Lawrence wrote:

> *I consider myself as the most wretched of men, full of sores and corruption, and who has committed all sorts of crimes against his King. Touched with a sensible regret, I confess to Him all my wickedness, I ask His*

forgiveness, I abandon myself in His hands that He
may do what He pleases with me. The King full of mercy
and goodness, very far from chastising me, embraces
me with love, makes me eat at His table, serves me with
His own hands, gives me the key of His treasures; He
converses and delights Himself with me incessantly,
in a thousand and a thousand ways, treats me in all
respects as His favorite. It is thus I consider myself from
time to time in His Holy presence.[115]

Yes, what a King, who does not "punish us for all our sins…
does not deal harshly with us, as we deserve" (Psalm 103:10
NLT)! "With unfailing kindness," He draws me to Himself, and
conversing with me says, "I have loved you…with an everlasting
love" (Jeremiah 31:3 NIV) and "you are precious and honored in
my sight" (Isaiah 43:4 NIV).

Don't you just feel yourself relaxing as you imagine sitting
at His table? You, who as Brother Lawrence described, whom the
King "treats in all respects as his Favorite." Yes, let's be quick to
confess, to run to Him for forgiveness and often "thus consider"
ourselves from time to time in His holy presence!

Reflection

Have you come to know your heavenly Father in this intimate way?

Conversation with God

Father, I abandon myself to You today. I ask You to forgive me
where I have failed and remind me that Your love for me is
unconditional and unending.

115 Brother Lawrence, "Practice of the Presence of God: The Best Rule of Holy Life,
   Second Letter," Christian Classics Ethereal Library, July 13, 2005, accessed November
   27, 2016, https://www.ccel.org/ccel/lawrence/practice.iv.ii.html.

Roadside Reflection

Final thoughts from a
seasoned traveler

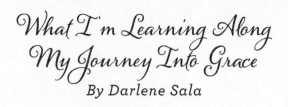

What I'm Learning Along My Journey Into Grace

By Darlene Sala

But grow in the grace and knowledge
of our Lord and Savior Jesus Christ.

2 PETER 3:18

I want to encourage you that the journey into grace is a long process, so don't get discouraged when you trip and fall along the way. The Lord is always near to help you on your way again. Here are a few things I'm still learning that might help.

1. **There is no substitute for reading God's Word.** I've tried skipping on days when I'm up to my neck in work. But I'm the loser. It's like skipping meals and still expecting to have the stamina you need for the day.

2. **My physical condition affects my spiritual condition.** Jesus knew the importance of rest. After the disciples had returned from an extensive ministry tour, Jesus knew they were exhausted, so He said, "Let's go off by ourselves to a quiet place and rest awhile" (Mark 6:31 NLT). I've also found that feeling "down" spiritually often comes at the same time I'm "down" physically. Don't be surprised.

3. **I need to keep ever before me the two great commandments Jesus gave us:**

* To love God with all my heart, soul, mind, and strength

* To love my neighbor as myself

Nothing else matters as much as these two commandments. Yet, it's so easy to forget to keep the "main thing the main thing." When I focus on these, everything else seems to fall in place.

1. **I need the kind of prayer time that is intimate**, not just a laundry list of requests. In her book *The Garden of Grace*, Jill Briscoe tells us to "take Heart Deep time with the Lord, where you just 'are' for a time until you are fully aware He 'is.' "[116] Making a connection with my heavenly Father is the most important part of prayer.

2. **Every night I need the Lord's invitation, "Come to Me, all who labor and are heavy laden, and I will give you rest" (Matthew 11:28).** I tend to carry my burdens to bed with me. Can you relate? That's why I love to hear God's voice at the end of the day inviting me to come to Him and receive the rest that only He can give.

Reflection

" 'For I am the LORD your God who takes hold of your right hand and says to you, Do not fear; I will help you' " (Isaiah 41:13 NIV).

Conversation with God

O Lord, help me—and my sisters on the path with me—to grow in our relationship with You as we journey into grace.

116 Jill Briscoe, *The Garden Of Grace* (Oxford, England: Monarch Books, a publishing imprint of Lion Hudson plc), 2007.

*Let us then approach God's throne of grace
with confidence,so that we may receive mercy
and find grace to help us in our time of need.*

HEBREWS 4:16 NIV